This book is dedicated to my king, my warrior, my hero: Grant Cardone. To my beautiful daughters, Sabrina and Scarlett, who inspire me every day. And to the legions of future empire builders out there — I am here to help you achieve the building of your empire. 10X!

Contents

Part One: Empire Builder 9
Part Two: Envision Your Empire 39
Chapter 1: Define Your Purpose: The Holy Grail 41
Chapter 2: The List 49
Chapter 3: Know Your Role: The King & Queen 63
Chapter 4: The Lotto Game 79

Part Three: Build Your Empire 85
Chapter 5: Get On The Same Page! 87
Chapter 6: Seek Your Own Counsel 99
Chapter 7: Say 'No' To Normal 109
Chapter 8: Sweat The Small Stuff 121
Chapter 9: Your Royal Court 131
Chapter 10: Lighten Up! 141

Part Four: Defend Your Empire 147
Chapter 11: Enemies Of The Empire 149
Chapter 12: How To Destroy An Empire 165
Chapter 13: Hold Down The Fort 171

Part Five: Expand Your Empire 183
Chapter 14: Be A Gold Digger 185
Chapter 15: Your Empire-Building Toolbox 195
Chapter 16: Beyond The Empire: Your Legacy 209

Acknowledgments 215
Resources 221
About Elena Cardone 225

"You are either building an empire or destroying one."
-Elena Cardone

PART ONE

Empire Builder

"A GREAT EMPIRE, LIKE A GREAT CAKE, IS MOST EASILY DIMINISHED AT THE EDGES."
—BENJAMIN FRANKLIN

My name is Elena Cardone and I am married to an extremely powerful self-made man, Grant Cardone. He is halfway to achieving a target (that I gave him) of hitting a billion dollars. Why did I give him a target so massive and so unattainable? You will find out but I assure you it certainly wasn't because I feel "entitled" to live a certain lifestyle to keep up with the Jones! No, as my friends will tell you, I'm most happy in my BDU's (Battle Dress Uniform) running down an obstacle course shooting targets on a gun range.

Grant is a New York Times bestselling author, the number-one sales trainer in the world, has five privately-held companies that have annual revenues exceeding $150 million and owns and operates a real estate portfolio valued at just under a billion dollars.

I want to shed light on my role as a woman from where I was to who I had to become in order to be "the woman behind/beside the man" and how we did it, and continue to do it together. My intention is to help any man or woman who is interested in creating a real legacy, and empire. If I can offer any guidance as to the do's and don'ts that will help fast-track your success, to eliminate the time it took us, then I feel obligated to share this information with you.

I have two web series. One I do with my husband, Grant which is a weekly series show called, *"The G&E Show"* (Grant & Elena) about the business of marriage, raising a family and building an empire. It also gives us a weekly project to work on as a couple and keeps us focused on our own accountability and dedication to our marriage. It's like we say on the show, *"We aren't perfect but we are figuring it out."* And for what it's worth, I think we are doing a darn good job of it.

In addition to this, I interview women for another web series called, *"Women In Power"* which is a show for women exploring and sharing information to empower other women. We discuss any and all topics relevant to the guests on the show. Both shows can be viewed on MyGCTV.com, on iTunes under Cardone Zone, or on YouTube.

Over the course of fifteen years, I've learned a thing or two about creating a rock-solid marriage — and keeping it together when everything is on the line. So much so, that if there's one thing I'm asked more than anything else, it's this, *"How do I get a relationship like you and Grant's?"* or, *"How can I get my husband to be more like Grant?"* Sometimes it's, *"How can I be more like you?"* While these are flattering questions, the answer is quite simple, you need to build an empire and you will have everything you ever wanted!

Start today. Not tomorrow. Not in a month from now. You have no time to waste.

What The Heck is An Empire?

Most people get images of antiquated kings and queens ruling empires from long ago with no reality whatsoever of how this can and does personally relate to them. If they do get the concept of a king or queen, many still misunderstand. They think it simply means to have the whole world centered around you, having life be easy, and having all the benefits of the world at your disposal.

Quite the contrary, when you truly are a king or queen and it's not just some title you have "declared" yourself on Instagram because it sounds important or noteworthy. When you actually choose to wear the crown, your responsibilities to people become more important than yourself. You will have to make tremendous sacrifices in order to grow your empire.

A king or queen actually serve their people and aren't afraid to work. They understand that it is necessary to do whatever it takes for the greater good in the name of the empire.

An empire is an operating system, a way of living that sets your purpose, morals, goals and values at the highest possible level, so that everything else in your life, from your career to the way you raise your kids, to the way you show up in your marriage, follows suit. It's based on the principle of self-governance and allows you to learn, grow and hold your ground in the best and worst of economic times.

Establishing, growing and defending our empire is how Grant and I have achieved colossal success thus far. It is the answer to all of those burning questions about how we do it all.

I wish I could tell you it will be easy. I wish I could tell you it will happen overnight. Hey, I wish I was a black belt in Brazilian jiu-jitsu. But let's face it, if I want that, I'd have to put in the work and years of training before that happens. Of course, building an empire doesn't happen overnight — nor did I begin my life riding around in private planes. Believe me!

> AN EMPIRE IS AN OPERATING SYSTEM: A WAY OF LIVING THAT SETS YOUR PURPOSE, MORALS, GOALS AND VALUES AT THE HIGHEST POSSIBLE LEVEL...

You MUST Build Your Empire

You are either building an empire or you are destroying one. This may be THE most important thing to know about empire building. Whether you know it or not, with every decision that you make each and every day, you are either creating or destroying your empire. You are either setting yourself up to win or you are holding yourself down. This applies to every decision from what you eat to the stupid fight you have with your partner. With every distraction that you partake in, you'll add time to your empire attainment.

An empire is the only thing that will ensure you and your loved ones can survive anything. Your empire is your saving GRACE. Empires can withstand massive attacks, fight wars and still manage to flourish through it all. However, a "normal" empire-less life in a normal world with unexpected catastrophes will simply crumble to ash.

Grant and I spent the first four years of our marriage being normal and having a normal "great" time. We were not thinking about building empires. We were content living in a beautiful home on the top of the Hollywood Hills with views overlooking downtown Los Angeles to Malibu. We had it made or so we thought. The who's who of Hollywood came to our house on the weekends. Grant's business was booming and I was working on primetime episodic TV. Life was good until the 2008 crash happened. And yes, it was a CRASH at my house.

The crash occurred along with a sixty-million dollar lawsuit from our "friends" (who actually conned us from the beginning). Neither Grant nor I had ever been involved in a lawsuit before. We were both a bit naive to the world of the rich back then. We didn't realize that con artists seek you out and you are just a mark with a big fat target on your back to them.

These people convinced us they were our friends and even had us be in their wedding! After Grant agreed to become partners with them, we found out they were a total scam and major liability to us. We had to release ourselves from that deal immediately. But the con had already been set at that point, and they thought they could get a good sixty million from us.

At the same time this was occurring and we were bleeding out hundreds of thousands in lawyer fees to defend ourselves against these cons, a belly-up bank wanted all their loan money back on our real estate portfolio. From 2008 to 2012, four hundred and sixty-five banks collapsed as a result of the economic crash. Banks were desperately trying to stay afloat and they needed money. So even though we had never been late on a payment to the bank, they declared since our net worth dropped (like everyone's in the entire country) that we were in technical default and wanted all the money now. I mean, who had fifty million liquid then?

As a middle-class girl from the streets of New Orleans who had never been around large amounts of money or exposed to such viciousness like this before, I knew I had to wake the hell up. The days of being oblivious were over if we were going to survive going forward. Grant's business as he knew it was over, and I was a few months pregnant with our first child. Try getting a job as an actress in LA while pregnant — yeah good luck with that!

There was an avalanche of stressful circumstances that no one plans for that hit us hard and fast. We were being attacked from every angle as desperate people stooped to desperate measures to get anything and everything we had. They were worse than vultures. Tensions ran so high between us, the temptation for Grant and me to explode on one another was immense. Then I realized something that would change our lives as a couple forever. I realized that Grant and I would have to use this catastrophe to fortify, unite together, and go fight the biggest war of our relationship together — side by side.

Let's face it, bad things happen to good people every day. Marriage is hard. Having kids is hard. Having no money is hard. Having money is hard. Winning is hard. Even playing the game of life is hard. But the hardest and most unbearable of all, is losing. If Grant and I had split up during those times, the enemies would have won. They would have destroyed our lives and that was just not an option. I HATE losing!

It took those darkest hours to get me to finally go ALL IN on myself and my marriage. I knew if I was going to survive this, I had to get behind Grant 100%. I didn't care who thought what of me or what women's group was going to "disown" me for supporting a man. I decided I was going to quit acting altogether and we were going to build an empire. We would never depend on someone or one source of income for our financial freedom ever again. It was difficult to visualize at the time but I knew if I got behind Grant with all of my power, resources and did whatever it took to back him, that we could rule our world.

I ran to tell Grant about my plans to expand us to wider depths than he ever imagined. I explained my "Empire" theory and how I would demand every ounce of fight he had in him and no matter what blood, sweat and tears he would shed, I would have his back every second of the way. I sold him somehow on my vision and he bought in. Then I asked him what he needed from me. His only response was, *"All spending stops."* I said, *"That's it?! DONE!"* I had the easy job.

For the next couple of years we went into "sacrifice" mode. We didn't spend a dime unless it went to build the business. We didn't go out on the weekends or do much of anything except work side by side day in and day out. There was something incredibly romantic though, knowing you have a bond with someone so powerful, that you refuse to let anyone or anything break you. To this day, we would fight to the death to defend and protect each other. Trust, honor and courage are what our foundation was built upon.

Building an empire is what saved us and it will save you. It will make everything else easier.

This book contains my "secrets" on how to build an empire, so that the other parts of your life — marriage, kids, career, the community you live in, your contributions to society, will all thrive. I wrote it with the hope of waking others up to the idea of bigger dreams and possibilities, of empires that spread and make a difference for the better, throughout the world.

Elena Rosaia

Before I became Mrs. Grant Cardone — or Ms. Elena Lyons, Hollywood actress — I was Elena Rosaia. Also know to only my dearest friends in New Orleans as Lane Rose. I guess I've had a few alias in my life. I was born in Spain as a U.S. citizen to a mom who worked at the U.S. Embassy and father, a World War II veteran who earned an income as a sporting clay shooter throughout Europe. We moved back to the States when I was one-year old because my mom missed her family and wanted us to be reared in U.S. They agreed to settle into New Orleans, one of the few cities my dad deemed "European enough" after having spent so much time overseas.

My father never found his footing once back in the States. He worked a job here and there but never anything that brought in any real income. My mom was the primary breadwinner and we very often lived paycheck to paycheck. We had periods of hard financial times and it tormented my father for years. He secretly resented my mother for making him move back to the U.S. where he gave up his fame and glory of being a European world champion shooter to being a jobless unknown in America. She secretly resented him for not being able to get and keep a job.

Both did good of trying not to show the financial stress we were under but I could always feel the undercurrent of constant worry and anxiety about money. I know it takes a toll on even the best of couples. Despite this, they were both extremely supportive, loyal partners and exceptional parents.

My father, Pops, wanted two boys but got two girls. I was the youngest so he made do. I was a complete tomboy until around the age of twelve. My passion for guns and acting both derived from him. He could imitate all kinds of voices and had dreamed of being a radio star. He was an actor by nature and such a character. For instance, my sister wanted Pops to pick her up from the movies a block away when she went through the "being embarrassed of your family" phase. Well, Pops wasn't having it. He got out of the car and acted like the Hunchback of Notre-Dame. He hobbled down the street yelling after my sister, "Cece", in his best, grotesque voice, *"Cece, it's your father."* She was mortified and tried to run away but Pops persisted, *"Come here, don't run away."* I was dying laughing and could not stop. It was so funny. He did a really good hunchback! I loved how uninhibited you could be by assuming a character and I wanted that freedom too.

I recall the exact moment I wanted to be an actress. I was nine years old sitting on the sofa watching a night-time TV show with my parents. The actors were holding each other's hands in an extremely dramatic love scene. They said to one another, *"No matter what I say. No matter what I do. I will always love you."* My father and I looked over at each other and died laughing. No one knew why we were laughing but we did. It was because the actors were so overly dramatic it was hysterical. We laughed so hard. Then we started to say it to each other as dramatically as they did it and we would laugh all over again. We did this for years and it became our inside joke and I associated acting with fun.

At nine years old, that moment of realization of what an actor does excited me. What an actor can do with a role and the number of ways they could play a scene intrigued me. It made me want to study people, their reactions and what was said versus what they did. I have been on a lifelong study of people ever since, and it isn't something I know how to shut off to this day.

Around ten to eleven years old, my father taught me to shoot shotguns. On the range with him and his buddies, I shot a 12-gauge and that alone would impress them. However, when I smoked clays, they would cheer and call me "Annie Oakley," and tell my father, *"Yep, she has your blood!"* They said it with such pride and I swam in the admiration. As a competition shooter today, it's safe to say that it was love at first click. A total daddy's girl I was and always will be.

My childhood was idyllic. Lots of time spent outside with neighborhood kids and the more down and dirty I was, the more I loved it. We would ride bikes, roller skate, hang at the park, play ball — kick ball, baseball, football, dodgeball. While it was easy to view the world through rose-colored glasses, around my fourteenth birthday, tragedy struck, and it permanently changed the way I experienced life.

Goldie

It was the start of my freshman-year of high school, and summer was still winding down. One night, very late into the evening, my father woke me up. Apparently, my best friend Goldie's house, which was across the street from ours, was on fire. He said, *"Goldie's house is on fire."* In my last attempts to peacefully hang onto any last shreds of an unscathed childhood I luckily had been bestowed, I refused to bat an eye. But it wasn't until I heard his next sentence that I was forever jolted out of bed and out of my innocent childhood forever, *"And Goldie and her mother are still in it!"*

We attempted to douse the fire by throwing buckets of water onto the flames and using garden hoses to spray water until the firemen showed up. Ultimately, we watched helplessly as Goldie's home was devoured by raging flames. There was no way anyone could enter without risking their own life.

By the time the sun began to rise, the fire department had extinguished the blaze but it was too late for Goldie and her mom.

A fireman recovered Goldie's limp body from the house. My father who was trying to shield me from having to witness the sight was holding on to me fortunately. Unfortunately, his attempt failed. The sight of Goldie's completely disfigured body from severe burns was more than I could comprehend. My knees buckled and I collapsed.

I'd never seen such a horrendous sight, nor experienced such deep, intense heartbreak.

I did come from a loving, but emotionally guarded home. My emotions were checked at the door. We always forged forward so the very next day, I somehow returned to school. I swallowed my pain. Sucked up the agonizing grief. By all outward appearances I never seemed phased — but on the inside, I crumbled and lost my will to live.

From that point on, I turned to drugs and alcohol for either of these three reasons: as a death wish, as a means to cope with the overwhelming loss or to maintain the "everything is just fine" facade. I made a decision that dreadful day that I would no longer feel emotions and did everything I could to numb my tormented soul. I enacted an icy wall of steel around my heart, determined to never let anyone or any vulnerable emotion inside that could hurt me again. This wall lasted I had created lasted for the next fifteen years.

From New Orleans to Los Angeles

High school and the French Quarter brought along its own special flavor. To cope with my excruciating loss, I delved into the punk rock scene. I found my family of misfits and adopted a character called "punk rock chick," which gave me an outlet to express my inner turmoil.

This was thirty years ago when punk was real punk and not mainstream or fashionable. I shaved the bottom half of my head and the top half was in big knots. You couldn't call it dreads because it wasn't in individual locks. It was more like if you picked up one piece of my hair, the whole head of hair lifted.

I would wear short skirts with the garter belt showing with ripped fish net stockings and white marching boots with a cropped torn t-shirt of some sort. I was doing punk rock things like slam dancing, stage diving and spray painting buildings. Yep, my tag name was "Sassy." One night, I spray painted a huge six-foot "SASSY" on the front of a Toys "R" Us that had a huge bright spotlight on it because I wanted my tag to be bolder and bigger than any of the guys' tags. And a week later after it had been removed, I had the audacity to do it again.

The guys and I would constantly challenge each other to the next, even more outrageous dare. I loved hanging with guys for two reasons; I felt they understood me the most and I was always guaranteed a rush. Nothing could ever top my New Orleans girls though. They are my ride-or-die for life.

In the French Quarter one night, the guys dared me to race this guy who I'll call Pink Mohawk, who I secretly had a crush on, to run atop the roofs of parked cars for an entire city block. You have no idea how exhausting it is to run drunk and high on top of car roof after car roof for an entire block but I did it. On the last car, I fell, slid off the hood and scrapped up my leg but I did cross the finish line first! I was also limping for the next week but that didn't bother me much.

Everything in those days was a dare. If there wasn't a punk rock show to go to at the VFW Hall, we would entertain ourselves by skipping out on restaurant bills, throwing bottles at buildings, tagging buildings, shoplifting, and riding in stolen vehicles — just to name a few of our recreational activities. All in the name of rebellious fun. One time, I was with the guys joyriding in a stolen car when the police pulled us over. They were about to arrest us all when the two guys I was with told the cop to let me go. They told him I didn't know the car was stolen. The cop asked me if I knew it was stolen and I said, *"Yes I knew."* He replied, *"I believe the guys"* and then he ordered me to walk home. Even amongst thieves, I have always surrounded myself with guys willing to protect me. It's a trait to this day that I don't take for granted.

I'm not proud of any of this but I was without a purpose, trying to escape the realities of life, and destroying any chance of building anything, much less an empire.

While New Orleans was a crazy kind of fun, it didn't hold a lot of potential for me. Not to mention, I could not bear having to see Goldie's burned out home across the street every single day.

Additionally, I had lost eight more friends — four in car accidents, one suicide, two overdoses, and one fell off a balcony. If I'd stayed, there was a high chance I'd wind up addicted to drugs, dead, or both — and the acting bug had already bit. I used acting to get me out of my high school. You see, I went to McMain Magnet Public High School from '88-'91. Back then the school was pretty rough.

First off, there was no air conditioning so it was hot and your shirt would be wet with sweat. Second, there would be dead roaches in the hallways and I hate roaches. Last, we would go on lockdown because the rival gangs from the school down the street would try to bum-rush our school. If the doors weren't locked in time, a massive fight would break out until the teachers or police would break it up.

Although I hated high school, I got along with everyone and had friends there too. Once, a new girl at school came up to me in chemistry class, threw her book down at my table and told me to find another stool. The girl next to me, who was from one the toughest housing projects in New Orleans, flashed a blade and told her to leave the crazy white girl alone. The girl grabbed her book, sat somewhere else, and I never had a worry or concern from anyone ever again.

When I asked the girl sitting next to me why she did that she said, *"You're cool. You're crazy, but you're cool. You make me laugh and you mind your own business. You didn't deserve that."*

Oddly, I was not scared when that happened to me, mainly because I didn't care where I sat and had no problem moving. However, the whole experience was quite profound for me. I admired the courage it took for that girl to stand up for me — the crazy white girl.

Nonetheless, when my sister told me how I could escape McMain, I jumped at the opportunity. She told me about a specialty school for the arts, NOCCA, the New Orleans Center for Creative Arts. She said it was a difficult school to get it into but if I did make it in for acting, I could get out of McMain around noon and drive to NOCCA to finish the rest of the day. I immediately auditioned and was accepted, which turned into my saving grace. NOCCA made my high school years bearable. The training I received turned into my ticket to Los Angeles. From my sophomore to senior high school year, I spent half of my academic school day at McMain and the other half at NOCCA.

At seventeen-years old and three days after my last high school exam, I moved to Los Angeles. I didn't even wait to graduate on stage. My parents begged me not to go as they thought I would get "peer pressured" into doing drugs. I sat them down and confessed it all. I said, *"Name a drug, any drug and I've done it."* Not cocaine though. Never did that one. That was the evil drug that turned my coolest of friends mean.

My mom worked for U.S. Customs, which among other things, searched for banned and illegal substances trying to be smuggled into the U.S. This of course included drugs. You can imagine her face when I proceeded to tell her about all the drugs I had taken, including accidentally growing two marijuana plants in our back yard. She was horrified and afraid her job was going to be in jeopardy, but I continued with my story.

I had a trampoline in my backyard and the neighborhood guys would come over and we all would clean our weed while hanging out on it. I haven't smoked pot or been around it in eighteen years but back when I was a teenager, the junk weed we smoked had twigs and seeds in it. You had to pick them out before rolling your joint and we would end up dumping the stems and debris over the side of the trampoline.

One day, one of the guys said, *"Oh wow, Lane Rose, your two marijuana plants are looking awesome!"* I had no idea I was even growing plants! I said, *"What are you talking about?"* He said, *"Look."* And lo and behold, growing in the midst of the overgrown lawn, were two six-inch marijuana plants.

Then I turned to my father and told him my mushroom story. I asked, *"Pops, remember the time, I had you pull over after we were done shooting? I had us crawl under a barbed wire fence into a cow pasture. You kick over cow manure patties as I picked those mushrooms with the dome-shape top (not the flat ones). We filled two one-gallon sized plastic bags filled with mushrooms for a science project?"* He replied, *"Yes, of course I remember."* Well, I confessed, *"That wasn't for a science project. Those were hallucinogenic mushrooms."*

I chopped them up into pint-sized pieces and mixed them in with several batches of sweetened iced tea. I had also added a pound of sugar to the batches because hallucinogenic mushrooms literally taste like poo. I went to the French Quarter that night and freely shared the tea with any willing participant. It seemed the entire French Quarter was shrooming. They called me the "Queen of the Quarter." This is NOT something I'm proud of. Today I realize how damaging drugs are on people — mentally, physically and spiritually.

By the time I was done telling all the gory details of not only these stories but so many others, they understood I had to get out of New Orleans. I convinced them my intentions were to clean up my act and make something of myself.

My time spent in theatre had given me enough gunpowder to nab an agent in Los Angeles. So at seventeen, with my parent's blessing, I moved out of their house and across the country and I never looked back.

For the next several years, I worked as a model and actress with the good fortune to travel to cool parts of the world. Although I didn't fully clean myself up, I was more focused and had tamed down quite a bit. I found myself hanging in LA's hot rod muscle car scene and shooting shotguns by day while I gallivanted in the Hollywood Celebrity scene by night.

I developed my passion for sixties muscle cars in Los Angeles. There was no shortage of gorgeous hot rods bumping around LA in the nineties. I loved the sound of those rumbling engines. These cars would taunt me with the sight of those mean grills staring me down, begging me to press the pedal to the metal, tires screaming, engines squealing, burning smoke as I accelerated out of a red light. It was invigorating to say the least! I was a total car junkie and I was hooked on the high. If some guy was at the same light in the car next and challenged me to a quick little race to see if I had the guts, I could never resist. Even if I lost, the look in guys' eyes when they stared at me with crazy astonishment and admiration was too addictive. The high was real and I jonesed for the rush. It also didn't hurt that the hot-rod guys were hotter than hell.

I couldn't get enough and wanted to learn everything I could about muscle cars which included working on them first hand. I wanted to do more than just be able to change a tire. I wanted to completely rebuild and restore these beautiful beasts. Over the next few years, the gearhead guys taught me everything I now know. They let me work side-by-side with them in the shop. I learned to replace brake pads, change a heater core (which is not as easy as it seems when you have to completely rip out the dash to get to it), install a distributor and whatever other task needed to be done. I discovered I became valuable for my little hands and my organizational skills.

See, I would label each and every part that I dismantled with a description on how it fit back together like a puzzle because I knew I would have no clue when it was time to reassemble the pieces. The guys would be amazed at how quickly I could get something back together. It became my strong suit. Anytime the guys needed me to get into a small space or needed help with how something went back together, they would call me over. *"Squirrel, come here"* they would say. They called me squirrel because they said my hands were as little and fast as a squirrel eating a nut.

I was continuously quizzed. They would see if I could diagnose hypothetical problems as well as randomly pointing to cars and seeing if I could guess the year based on my car history knowledge. I could determine the year fairly quickly based on a few characteristics such as if the car had smoker windows or not, round or square wheel wells, by the front grill or rear tail lights. I was never off by more than a year if I was ever wrong at all. They would always give me that side look with a chuckle when I answered correctly and I loved making them proud.

Under their supervision, I tricked out my very own prized possession — a convertible '65 Chevelle Malibu RS SS. It was red with a black interior which I upholstered myself. I traded an entire car, my Toyota Tercel, for a 350 engine with a high-performance cam and replaced the entire engine in my own car. It was a proud moment for me. Before I drove it home, the NASCAR guys that helped me said, *"Break her in hard if you plan to race her."* So, from Barstow to Los Angeles, I drove 110-120 miles per hour. I was so terrified I'd be pulled over by cops. I had never sped that fast in my life. My legs were trembling so badly, it looked like I was channeling the spirit of Elvis. Ever since, I've had a pretty sick love affair with hot rods.

Then there were my shotgun buddies who were quite a bit older than me. They acted like I was their little sister and tried to protect me from all the bad boys — which of course never existed. However, I always loved the idea of having an over-protective brother and I found that in these guys. I felt so comfortable around them and relaxed while shooting. I loved being outdoors just competing against myself. Every time I would break a clay or smell that gunpowder, I would feel an intoxication like no other. It was a calm and peaceful kind of rush, that at the same time, released an aggression I had been harboring since my teens. I inherited the love of shooting from my father and I'm convinced it more than just runs through my veins, it's in my DNA.

These gems of gentlemen had me shooting sporting clay good enough to take 10th female in California. And this was before I actually had formal training by three-time world champion Dan Reeves.

However, being one of the only girls with the most bitchin' ride in all of LA (who actually talk about cars), who hot rodded through town, shot shotguns, was a single model/actress, who could also out-drink most men, well, some of the guys in any one of all these scenes would make the unfortunate mistake of becoming infatuated with me. From time to time for fun, I would date one of them. I admit I was a bit boy crazy and would go weak for a cute guy. However, I always forewarned them that I wasn't interested in being in a serious relationship and please, for the love of God, do not fall in love with me. It would be an absolute disaster. The more they would want a relationship, the more I wouldn't. Looking back, I can see why I was addicted to adrenaline. Void of any deep emotional feelings for anyone, I craved that rush to feel alive and bust up the numbness that I felt in my heart.

I was terrified. Relationships equaled loss of freedom to me and I had a streak in me that couldn't be tamed. It would not stop and it went full throttle all the time. I could not stay in and just chill because that felt like death. I had to always be on the go and onto the next project. It drove guys nuts that I couldn't be content with just them. The more they tried to stop me, the more I felt I had to get away, always on the run. It literally felt like I could not breathe and that I was going to die if they stopped me. Men equaled "holding me back" and suffocation. I hated to seem arrogant and I hated even more to be cruel but I always ended the romance at this point.

If one of them ever cried, it killed me. I just wanted to have fun and never meant to hurt anyone. I completely understood what was going on when my girlfriends would cry to me over a guy. I would tell them guys are no different than girls. Guys feel pain just like girls do when they got hurt. There were plenty of good guys out there. They just needed to find the one who was mature enough and ready to be in a relationship rather than trying to change the person who was dead set against it. I spoke from experience. I hated when I saw my girlfriends suffer over some loser guy. And, I hated being that loser chick that would do the same thing but no guy stood a chance of ever getting through. EVER.

Don't get me wrong, I adored men. I have never been a man-hater. Quite the contrary, everything I ever wanted, as far as my dreams went, a man helped me achieve it. The greatest love you can give someone, and I have said this before, is to help someone achieve their goals. Men, whether in a platonic relationship with me or more, have shown me that love. Every goal and dream I ever had, it was a guy that had the patience to teach me how. Every single mentor I've ever had, aside from my mother, was a guy. I have the utmost respect for men. Real men, who love and protect women, were my buddies. There was always mutual respect and I appreciated all they did for me. But to give one of them my heart, oh hell no.

I starred in dozens of commercials which paid the bills until I booked a great gig, USA High For more than three years and ninety-five episodes, I was on an international hit TV show that was similar to Saved by the Bell. Everywhere I went I was recognized by teens and preteens from around the world. The money was unbelievable for a girl from New Orleans. I bought a house, a couple more cars. I even wholly supported financially the boyfriend I finally decided to "get serious with" as I attempted to fit into the relationship world. He couldn't afford anything but I was OK with that. I didn't want to owe anyone anything and didn't ever want some guy thinking he could control me. My theory was, if I have my own money I always had an escape route. I was very independent to say the least.

Sidenote: The women's movement had a firm hold on my thinking at that time. I was convinced by Hollywood nonsense that "a strong woman must earn her own money, pay her own way and never depend on anyone." Such nonsense. As I look back, the Hollywood industry is built on people depending on others. The actress and the actor depend on a manager, on an agent to make a contract, a writer for a script and the entire structure of Hollywood for any chance for to work at all.

Bottom line is I learned how to fend for myself. I paid my own bills and wouldn't let anyone take care of me. I was that independent woman the media had me convinced was the goal. At that time, I had no concept of building an empire, flying private, traveling the world or controlling my own destiny. I had absolutely no interest in being married, having children or that one day I could somehow influence the lives of millions.

From LA to Love in an Unexpected Place

In comes Grant Cardone, which I share later in more detail, but for now, a crash course.

Girl moves to LA. Finds work as an actress. Finds a handful of men not worth the time of day. Girl starts to question her life. Seeks self-improvement courses. In turn, meets a handsome, successful, confident man, who is new to town — and with whom she wants nothing to do.

Man, undeterred by girl's behavior (including not returning the man's twenty-six phone calls over thirteen months), works his way into her inner circle and uncovers girl's first love — guns. Boy calls girl and states he has rented out an entire shooting range in LA for the two of them. Girl agrees to a date (even though it's not really a date). Slowly, but surely, and with much trepidation, the girl begins to allow the man into her world... and her heart.

Man, aware of his incredible good fortune, wastes no time in proposing to girl (which girl, at first, thinks is a joke). Girl, eventually realizing her good fortune in having found the exact man she'd once hoped for, comes to her senses. The pair marries, have children, leave Los Angeles, and set off for a new life 3,500 miles away in Miami,

Florida, with plans of reaching seven billion people and dominating the world together as one cohesive empire.

You know, just your everyday, run-of-the-mill love story.

PART
TWO

Envision Your Empire

"Everything you can imagine is real."
—Pablo Picasso

Chapter

1

Define Your Purpose: The Holy Grail

Your purpose is who you are to your core. It is the Holy Grail, also known as your "why", and your reason for getting out of bed in the morning. For some of you, your spouse or kids might immediately spring to mind. For others, you might think of your job, and what sort of role you play there. These are all important pieces of your empire, but your purpose has to be so big, so wide, so gravitational, that even if you were sick, injured or seriously questioning your commitment to continue, it would give you the type of inner strength needed to blow past any doubts, temptations, or distractions.

When you connect with your purpose, you'll find that it's easier to discipline yourself to do the difficult things or to make the right choices when kicking back or quitting seems like a better option. You know you have a good solid purpose if you have ever experienced life roughing you up around the edges for a while, but before you threw in the towel, that little voice of reason said, *"Maybe you can keep going, even just for another hour."* That was your purpose and it gave you the strength to pull yourself up yet again and put one foot in front of the other.

Invisible Armor

Battles are inevitable. On the micro scale there are bad days. Whether it's a stupid fight with a loved one or with a coworker in a boardroom. On the macro scale, they include recessions, depressions, corporate devastation and actual war. While preparing for battle or whether you are engaged in a full-on assault, the one item you must "wear" no matter what the season, is your purpose. It serves as a type of armor and keeps your empire intact when everything else seems to be falling apart. This will also act as a guideline. You will be able to recognize when you need to back down from a silly argument that leads nowhere. You will start to recognize distractions as simply that, a distraction, and you will avoid falling into those pitfalls. You will soon get over your avid craving to be "right" all the time. You'll learn to start acknowledging the situation for what it is while continuing to move forward. FYI, when you can do this with a genuine smile, you have become a bona fide master.

When you are clear about who you are and where you want to go, putting your ego aside for the greatest good will become easier. You will be amazed how much free time you will have on your hands when you stop fighting ridiculous battles all in the name of trying to get someone to see your side and agree you are right. Again, it is NOT your purpose to be the righteous "know-it-all."

Fight the wars of true injustices when they rear their ugly head. Fight the war against the enemies of positive change. Fight the war to make a difference for the better in this world. Those are the battles worth the pain and suffering. Your loved ones are not the enemy. If they are, you need to go play bigger games. Get an enemy or two, and fight on the same side together. Knock off the silly little games you've been playing with each other. You know they are too small and beneath you. Don't be average. Give yourself a challenge and go create a dynasty. That is what you were born to do.

Our Purpose: An Empire of Seven Billion People

Just so you get an idea of just how big a purpose can be Grant and I have our main goal as a couple to reach and help all seven billion people of earth. Is this target ridiculous? Unattainable? Yes, and it's just what we need to keep us motivated and occupied for a very long time!

My own personal purpose is to help others have the reality and know-how to create an empire. This isn't just for the select few. I'd love for everyone to understand the value of a partnership and the workings of relationships — whether in business or in marriage. Couples need to be on the same page in order to build their empires. They can't go to the office all day to build, only to come home and destroy it, and expect to amount to anything worthwhile. I also want to disrupt the noise of the mainstream media that portrays marriage as uncool and boring.

Ideally, if I eliminate the learning curve for others or fast-track their success in life, then I have fulfilled my mission. I will have the gratification of knowing that "little ole" me actually made the world better for having been in it. This is the legacy I want to be known for.

In addition to that, my husband's educational materials aim to train people to become financially self-sufficient so they have the ability to take care of themselves and their families. I stand behind/beside Grant because I support his message and his mission which ultimately aligns with mine as well.

Collectively speaking, Grant and I want to use our own lives as a chalkboard of sorts. You can see where we've gone wrong (and avoid those same avenues of pain) and where we went right so that you can rocket your way to success.

It's big. It's bold. It says a lot about who I am. Some might say it's delusional or over the top, but it's mine. And just as I'll defend my empire, I'll defend my purpose, too.

Stay Strong

I'm nowhere near achieving the goal I just mentioned. Yet every day, I "suit up," and try my best to remain fearless. When things don't seem to be progressing as quickly as I'd like, I don't drop my purpose, lower my target, or pick a new one. I simply form mini-targets that I can actually hit in the meantime.

Here's another secret as to what keeps me on track — hearing from you guys, our fans who we call our family. I absolutely love to read your success stories and hearing just how far we've reached. You remind me of the importance of us living up to our personal code of conduct, and that our efforts are worth it.

Life, however, doesn't present itself in one straight-and-narrow line. In fact, it's the twists and turns that make it so interesting, and I wouldn't trade in any of our hard times for easy streets. I learned a lot about the kind of character both Grant and I have when things seemed grim. Again, it's purpose that will light up those dark alleys when you're not sure where to turn next, and purpose that will gently nudge you to stay on track when a distraction seems too good to pass up.

Set Yourself Up to Win

You've got to prepare yourself for the inevitable bumps and bruises that lie ahead. Having a mindfulness or spirituality can be enormously helpful. For others, regular exercise can help align your body and mind when it comes to building inner and outer strength. It's extremely important to set smaller, sub-targets for yourself that you can hit while paying the dues on the much bigger targets that don't happen overnight. I shoot guns and train in martial arts not only because it gives me a sense of confidence but it also doubles as an achievable target I can accomplish in the interim.

When you are feeling overwhelmed by how long things seem to take, what you need is a good win. Be sure to give yourself challenging but achievable targets so you feel a sense of success from these smaller wins that will motivate you while your dreams come to fruition.

Empire-Building Exercise: Define Your Purpose

Envision the kind of purpose you'd set for yourself and your empire when you're feeling on top of the game. Imagine one of those days where everything went right, you felt you ruled the world, and you achieved everything easily. Odds are, you would raise the bar a lot higher than you would if you felt like your feet were dragging and everything was holding you back.

And that's just it, you've got to create this massive purpose so on the days your heels are sticking in the mud, you've got the tenacity to keep pushing through. You have to know that no opposition is going to hold you down.

Allow your mind to go there. It might feel ridiculous to think so big when we have all been conditioned to be grateful and content with where we are. There are well-intentioned good people all over the world who were raised to think small. Even though they're adults, they've settled so far into the status quo they have a hard time in changing their mindset. Don't fall into this category. Define your purpose.

This exercise when done properly, will galvanize your motives and help you reach your full potential. You will soon see the benefits of your bigger purpose when your life improves. The smaller things (and even people) will no longer bother you. You will have more energy to stay focused and produce at higher echelons.

Chapter 2

The List

Before I became Mrs. Grant Cardone, I was Ms. Elena Lyons. An unencumbered, oh-so-cool, take-no-prisoners Hollywood-dwelling actress who, like many women today, was exhausted and unimpressed by the modern dating scene.

Many of you reading this might already be familiar with the story of how I met Grant — or at least his version of how we met. For the most part, it's true. He'd just moved to LA from San Diego, and somehow, wound up on the set of a commercial in which I was starring. Despite the policy of not sharing actors' private information, he persuaded his friend, the director, to give him my number. He called me and it made me so upset that my number had been given out. He proceeded to tell me that people's lives tend to improve who hang out with him. I thought to myself this has to be the most arrogant guy of them all. By the time I hung up the phone, I absolutely loathed him.

For the next year, he proceeded to call me twice a month, every month — even though I wasn't interested, and returned none of his calls. Grant continued to work his way from the outside in and found out that I was into guns. My weakness. My kryptonite. The next message I got from him (and in those days, we had answering machines) was an invitation to join him at a shooting range. He'd booked the entire thing just for the two of us and wanted to know if I was interested... Uh, like a bee to honey... yeah, I went! I know, I hate that I'm so predictable too.

Still, it took several months of being friends before any sort of real romance blossomed. Sure, I had a healthy dose of skepticism after having lived for a decade in the land of shiny, empty promises. Mostly, it was because of my history of staying emotionally detached. Grant persisted, remaining patient and committed while I slowly unfolded into the relationship, allowing my tough exterior to slip away as I began to trust, and eventually fall in love.

But what you don't know is that before I met Grant, he existed metaphorically on paper, on what I call "The List" before he physically showed up.

The Magical, All-Encompassing List

It's likely that you've heard of "The List" or some version of it. You write down all of the qualities you want in your potential partner, right down to their hair color, height, food preferences and even the kind of clothes he or she wears. "The List" allows you to get honest about your true desires. For example, it might seem shallow (or scary) to openly acknowledge that you want someone who's rich and successful or someone who can provide for a family no matter what the economy is doing. When I did my list I was so ashamed to write that I wanted a financially independent guy I wrote "Could afford to buy me a Cartier if he wanted."

I'd only had two "real" relationships and I financially supported them both. Neither guy could handle a woman being the bread winner. It takes a strong man and true teammates that know their roles in the relationship to make that role reversal work. But it can be done. Both guys later confessed it killed them that I could financially do what I wanted when I wanted without needing them for anything. I found out after I broke up with each that both had cheated on me.

One admitted that he cheated because he knew I would eventually break up with him and he wanted to hurt me before I hurt him. That was shocking to hear as I didn't know people thought like that. The other one confessed he cheated because he knew he wasn't the "man." He knew he would never be seen as the man in my eyes. As messed up as I was, I never cheated. It was a painful pill to swallow but their logic actually made sense to me.

I was exhausted from financially supporting men and vowed never to do it again. The last one refused to move out of my house when I broke up with him. He went further by threatening to put a mechanic's lien on my home if I attempted to sell it. He did all the labor to remodel my kitchen and felt after he had lived in my home (for free for over a year) that I now owed him for his kitchen remodel labor. That's when I decided I needed a real man who could create enough financially in his own life that he wouldn't need to steal from mine. That relationship ended with me signing over my home with the promise from him to never contact me again. I gave up a home that is worth over a million dollars today. It sucked back then but I learned you have to be willing to give something up in order to go build an empire.

I chalked it up as my fault for picking this guy in the first place. I walked away with my head held high, knowing I had what it took to recreate that and a whole lot more! After all, I was free and I could finally breathe again. Hence, if the perfect man could afford to purchase a Cartier watch for me, it somehow meant he had his own finances. For a change, I was ready to see what it felt like to financially have nice things done for me. I was DONE taking care of boys.

Ironically, when Grant and I started to hang out as friends, he put a watch on my wrist. He said I looked good wearing a man's watch and said I could wear it as long as I wanted. I never wore jewelry back in those days and didn't know one piece from the other. I did rather liked this watch though so I wore it. I should probably make up some romantic story here about how this next part actually went down but here's what really happened. One night, I was in a public restroom squatting over the toilet peeing (like girl's do in public restrooms) when I looked down at my arm and saw that the watch I was wearing was a Cartier!

I immediately thought of my "List" and went into a mild panic attack. My heart started pounding as I broke out into a sweat. I felt that shortness of breath coming on and knew I had to get that watch off as fast as I could. My internal thoughts were screaming, *"Grant is NOT my guy! He couldn't be THE guy. Why of all the watches I had to like, this one turned out to be a Cartier watch? Was this some sort of sign the universe was playing a sick joke on me? Did this act as a jinx for the real guy that was supposed to give me a Cartier watch?"* I was beyond freaked out!

I emerged from the bathroom stall frantically tearing at my wrist trying to unfasten the straps. While mumbling to myself, I stumbled to the sink to splash cold water on my face. A lady at the next sink asked me if I was ok. When my eyes met hers, it struck me like a bolt of lightning and I blurted out, *"It's a loaner! It's a loaner! Yeah I'm fine. Thank you."* I relaxed and took comfort in the fact that he had not actually given me a Cartier watch. Sigh of relief, it was a loaner.

Creating My List

Your list is a private pact between you and the universe, shared only with your inner circle if you so choose.

In my case, it was my friend who'd witnessed the frustrations in my "relationship" life, and who seemed dismayed when I told her that, at twenty-eight years old, I was done with dating. I vowed to be single forever once I'd broken up with Milquetoast. Being permanently single, I reasoned, was the best solution and one that I was clearly content with. However, my friend who was not so enthused about this idea, told me to get out a piece of paper and pen. She insisted that I write my "List." "The List" was everything that I wanted in the perfect man. If I had this man, I would want to be in a relationship with him permanently. The idea seemed far-fetched but I've never been one to back down from a challenge.

As I began to write, something in me began to stir. I felt excited at the prospect that there might be a man out there who matched up with this ideal guy. As you know by now, I was never the kind of girl who fantasized about what kind of wedding she'd have one day but "The List" was different. I felt like, who knows? Maybe if this man exists, I could be with him for the rest of my life. Nah, probably not, but here goes anyway.

Here's a sampling of what was on my "List":

- Be 6'2"
- Have green eyes
- Heterosexual (She said to be specific and being from crazy town, New Orleans, I thought I better include it.)
- A real man who protects women and children
- Single — NOT married
- Masculine
- Monogamous
- Drug-free
- Ethically ambitious
- Loves his mom and sisters (If he has any.)
- Never tries to control me
- Has a house in the Hollywood Hills
- Loves cars
- Can afford to buy me a Cartier watch if he wanted
- Self-confident and fun to be around
- Loves guns
- My friends and family love him
- He has my back no matter what and treats me with respect
- We laugh and love together
- He's healthy
- He's romantic
- He's honorable and courageous
- He always wants to better himself
- He inspires me to be the best version of myself
- He has hair on his head but not on his butt or back
- He dresses well and has good hygiene
- Incredible sex every time with beautiful private parts. (I had to put that one on the list. If you're like me, you cannot leave that one out.)

But the funniest thing happened. As I continued to write over one hundred items on the list I started to wonder if this guy actually did exist. What would his list of this "ideal" woman look like? That's when it occurred to me. His list would not look like my current condition. That's when I realized I had to objectively write "The List" from my perfect man's perspective to see exactly how far off-base I was. So that's what I did and this is a bit of what it looked like.

- Beautiful
- Loyal
- Drug and Alcohol-free
- Has her own life but cares about me
- Healthy and fit
- Intelligent
- Faithful and ethical
- Goes with the flow
- Nurturing
- Loves children
- Supportive
- Feminine
- A true partner. Helps me reach my highest potential
- Dependable and trustworthy
- Takes care of herself
- Has a positive outlook on life
- Wants a serious relationship and is interested in marriage
- Makes me feel proud to not only be "the man" but "her man"

While I had a few of those qualities already under my belt, I still had a lot of work to do on myself in order to become an asset to any man worth his salt. Given again, that I had nothing else to lose, I decided to invest in becoming a better version of myself through clean living, taking spiritual classes, and cutting toxic people and habits out of my life for good. After all, I already reasoned that I'd be just fine as a single gal. Even if this "List" business didn't pan out, I'd still get something from my self-improvement quest.

Truth be told, I met Grant only a month after I had written the list but hated him pretty much at first sight. He was a short, arrogant business guy who dressed like a golfer. I was used to dating rock stars covered in tattoos or movie stars with motorcycles. I had never dated a businessman. We had been hanging out for months as friends and Grant had made it known that he wanted to be with me but he never crossed the line. He patiently waited until I would one day have that epiphany about him being the one but I forewarned him that would never happen.

I finally told my "List" friend about my mini panic attack in the ladies room when I discovered the watch Grant had let me wear was a Cartier, quickly noting, it was a loaner. Because it was not given to me, I assured her I was safe. However her eyes got as big as saucers as she muttered to herself proudly, *"I knew it!"* She explained, *"Grant loves you and he did give you the watch."* She continued, as I looked at her perplexedly, *"He would give you the world if you let him. He had to say it was a loaner because he knew you are too much of a freak and wouldn't have worn it under any other circumstance."*

"You realize that Grant is the guy on your list," she said excitedly.

"No way, don't be ridiculous," I said.

"Elena," she said, *"read your list out loud to me."*

And so I started, *"6'2", green eyes, heterosexual, protects women and children, single, masculine, drug-free and ethically ambitious…"*

After I read every single item she said this, *"Elena, if you leave off his height and eye color — the two most insignificant items on your list — Grant is every single one of those things."*

I started to shake my head "no", when I realized she was right.

This time there was no panic attack.

Coming to Terms With My Equal

"The List" made me realize I always expected greatness from my relationships, but I wasn't giving greatness myself, including in my platonic and professional relationships. Things with Grant moved super slowly in comparison to my past relationships. I liked that we hung out as friends for several months. I felt comfortable around him and respected that he had made his true intentions and feelings for me known but never crossed the line or put me in that uncomfortable situation where you have to politely reject them or make up some story why you aren't interested in them. I had never met a man like Grant and a secret part of me liked the fact that he was making a genuine effort to get to know me — the real me, who honestly, I was figuring out myself. Grant was a kind and patient man who eventually became my rock, even though I tried to test his resolve.

I'd lived my whole life in flight, always in motion, never staying in one place for too long. My New Orleans girlfriends, who had seen it all, called me the "Great Houdini" because I could vanish from anyone or anything at the drop of a hat. If I ever told them I had a crush on a guy, they would shake their heads, feeling sorry for the luckless soul. I would say, *"No, I really like this one,"* but they gave me the cold hard facts and said, *"Lane Rose, boys have always been toys for you. You have never loved and you have never had your heart broken. You "Houdini" every guy who ever stands a chance."* And I tried all my "Houdini" tricks on Grant trying to avoid capture yet he always remained there, unfazed, with open arms. Actually, he even seemed rather amused by it all. That was a first.

He was the only man who ever was a beat ahead of me. I wasn't able to slip away. He was the only one who ever understood me. *"You know that monster that lives inside of you?"* he asked me. *"It's only about this big."* He held a one-inch space between his thumb and his forefinger. It was an overwhelming realization. I laughed to disguise that my eyes filled with tears. I had always thought that monster living within was bigger than I ever perceived my own self to be. In no way could it ever be destroyed. The fact that I had just been made by Grant Cardone, cut through me like a sword. For the first time in my life, it occurred that maybe Grant was right about my inner-demons being so small. And I was struck by the possibility of true love.

One night, at dinner, it hit me like a ton of bricks that I could no longer avoid the inevitable and I point-blank asked him, *"Are you going to make me fall in love with you?"* He said, *"Yes, yes I am."*

I literally responded, and please pardon the language, *"Oh, fuck."*

"Listen, Elena," Grant said, *"I promise for the next three days, thirty days or thirty years, that I will love, respect, cherish and be monogamous to you for as long as you let me. Will you be my girlfriend?"* I felt like I was in the sixth grade with that question. I was terrified, and he knew it. *"Three days?"* I said, *"Okay. I can do that. Yeah, I'll be your girlfriend."* Grant kissed me for the first time and we've been together ever since.

Empire-Building Exercise: Write Your List

Write your own list and hold nothing back. Be specific, but keep in mind the important non-negotiables such as character traits versus the "nice to have" line items such as being 6'2" and green eyes. Getting hung up on that alone cost me thirteen months don't forget.

This is especially important if you're used to the concept of falling in love or lust at first sight, and allow your emotions to sway your vision from a partner who's better suited for the long term. Remember, you are not "entitled" to this partner just because you and your friends tell you that you deserve this. It is equally as important to do the next part.

Write the list your ideal potential partner would want in their ideal mate. Identify the areas of your life that need improvement, and get started on a plan to make the necessary changes.

Married couples, you can still make a list or lists. Write out ways your husband or wife can help you further build your empire. For example, write the positive contributions you would like to see just as you would on the "The List." Don't write everything the other person is doing wrong and use the list as a fault finding, shame session. Rather look how you can each start working on ways to produce or deliver what is wanted from the other's list. And just how the single folks will be working on improving themselves, this will also be a time to look how to improve yourself and really become an asset to each other and to the empire.

The purpose of "The List" is to make you clear about who you are, where you want to be and what you want in your life. So be honest. Confront the existing scene in order to get the ideal scene you ultimately desire.

Chapter 3

Know Your Role: The King & Queen

At the top of the empire rests the king and queen, also known as emperor or empress, who lay out the rules of the land.

When I say *"know your role"*, what I really mean is you have to take ownership of living at a higher level. In building an empire, your mindset is half the battle. You have to be willing to not only think big but believe in things that might not yet be in your physical domain. Therefore, as king and queen, you have to carry yourself the way a king or a queen would. Even before you have technically earned the title and even before others see you as such.

First, let's start with the lady of the queendom, The Queen herself.

The Queen: Brilliant, Multifaceted, And Often Underestimated

Despite a feminine, soft, and often compassionate exterior, the queen must be the strongest, toughest, smartest, and most disciplined person in the empire. Her role is vital to the king. She hustles behind the scenes to secure allies, assets, and transactions that contribute to the good of the empire. The queen is trained in the art and science of life. She understands that life is a game and that the better she understands the rules, the better she will rule. She seeks to improve her skills and works through continued education, learning, and training.

A queen is self-aware. Awareness takes time to hone and develop. Once a queen develops this practice, however, nothing can stop her. The ability to read people and various situations will aid her in dodging life's bullets while conquering new territories. With a queen by a king's side, life for the royal couple is an adventure.

A queen inspires, possesses dignity, pride, grace, and is willing to put herself on the line for the sake of defending her king, and her empire. She knows that when she goes to battle for her court, they too, will battle for her out of mutual loyalty and respect.

The queen is a force to be reckoned with but she certainly doesn't take her power for granted. Rather, she uses it to improve the quality of life for everyone who matters to her. A queen seeks success by obligation and not for vanity purposes. It's done out of kinship, the queen knows that it's only when everyone within the empire succeeds that they can all reach their true potential together.

Queens Take Ownership

A queen isn't a princess. She's a woman. She's experienced her share of life's ups and downs, but has forged through each and every challenge thrown her way and emerged more determined and prepared for whatever shows up next. She knows what she wants, and goes after it without apology.

Queens are served by their kings, but it's not about racking up a closet full of shoes or being taken out to dinner once a week (though those things are nice, too). It's about knowing she's his equal, and when he serves her, he serves the entire empire by making sure she can reign at her highest and best self. Your king is there to complete you, not scrape you off the sidewalk you can't seem to ever peel yourself off of. Life is meant to be an adventure — not something that constantly knocks you around. You've got to show up as an active participant, not someone who rides around in the back seat, waiting for things to be handed to her.

Because here's a hard truth. No one in your empire will serve a fake queen. Heck, no one will even want to be around you if you've somehow associated being a queen with being a spoiled brat. What's sadder, and more humbling, is that if you're not fully aware of how you show up in this world and take 100% ownership of who and what you are, flaws, strengths and all — I guarantee you'll be knocked off your throne faster than you had a chance to sit on it.

Don't believe me? Have a look around at some of the divorces out there. What caused it, or rather, whom? Who in the empire sought to execute her? The divorce wasn't simply caused by what happened in the marriage. That was just a cover story for the insidiousness of the true nature of the one(or thing) that took her out! I guarantee, IEDs (Improvised Explosive Devices), metaphorically speaking, were placed all throughout that marriage waiting for the "happy couple" to blow themselves up.

If she acts like an entitled spoiled brat, no one will fight for her. And there will be no way she will have the stamina to defend herself against such vicious savages for any length of time. Like I said, it takes intelligence, dignity, integrity and power to run an empire. Ultimately, she is responsible for pulling her weight. An empire is built upon a strong foundation, and that is something that starts with her.

A Queen Pays Attention

One of my greatest strengths is the ability to observe. It's a skill that if you don't already have it, you must make it a priority to learn. Do whatever it takes to start to pay attention in your everyday life, including how you speak to and treat yourself (especially all you single ladies).

If you think being a queen is all about being lucky — well, you're wrong again. A queen creates her own luck. She even creates her own roll by dedicating herself to mastery. She'll make it look beautiful, fun, sexy and easy along the way. Fellow queens recognize and appreciate one another, knowing that the art of royalty comes with great sacrifice. But it's always, always worth it.

If you truly want to reign at the top of your empire, there's no other way to exist. The queen through her intense observation will know the character of all in her court. She's got to cut out those negative influences or else they will rule her instead of the other way around.

She will place the most honorable and loyal next to the king. She will find clever ways of eliminating the weak and no one will ever suspect it was her. She is not a troublemaker. She quietly and viciously protects the king. However, this is not to be confused with jealousy. She has way too much class and dignity. Nor would she ever create such drama. She has solutions and solves her own problems with minimal interference to the king or to the empire.

After all, if she has perfected and mastered her skills, everyone has been hand-picked or approved by her. She is then ultimately responsible for all internal operations relating to the empire. Her true talent is that she does all of this and so, so much more. Yet on the surface, it appears effortless and even coincidental.

Her life will appear to be only for the lucky few who happen to have the good fortune of having the "perfect" life. To the outside world, it might appear that she does nothing but to the king and the select few, they will always understand, respect, and appreciate her value.

In the beginning of our marriage, I definitely was not a queen and I made lots mistakes. For starters, I gave up my passion, shooting guns. Not because Grant asked me to, but I thought it would not be appropriate for me to shoot guns with the guys on the weekends being in a relationship. The problem was, I gave up an outlet that fulfilled me in a way that no one else ever could. Suddenly, I turned to Grant to fill that void. I wanted him to want to spend all of his spare time with me. I have never told him in our entire relationship to come home or not be late in any matters concerning business. However, Grant had another agenda with his free time. His twin brother lived a few doors down from ours and every evening they would get together and play Xbox until midnight.

As a recent newlywed who was not accustomed to men not wanting to be with me, it was a maddening experience. I was home alone, going to bed alone, questioning my marriage and what I had just gotten myself into. I felt so lost and confused as to how to make a marriage work. I always left in the past when things were no longer fun and this was not fun! Being on this side of the fence was awful. I turned into the person that I always loathed — desperate and needy.

Trying to solve my problem, I asked Grant if he could come home earlier. That turned out to be a disaster and got me nowhere. So I decided to ask his brother if he could send Grant home earlier. The more I wanted their help on this matter, the worse it got. They stayed out even longer and I was convinced they were conspiring against me. Remember, I wasn't a queen and no one wants to help an entitled princess.

In my thirties, I finally understood how I had made others feel for the first time in my life. Deep compassion and understanding emotionally for what others experienced now embodied my spirit and became very real to me. It occurred, that in order for this marriage to work, I would have to fulfill my side of the deal. Finding my own self and not depending on someone else to make me feel or be a certain way in order to have an identity, became my new path. If I found my real purpose and got so busy creating it, I would not have time to be so demanding of my husband's time. Once I did this, I knew I would become an asset to the relationship.

More importantly, I would have to do this for me, and for us, and not as a "Houdini" or payback. Trust me, I was tempted to get even and go out clubbing but I knew I had to grow up instead. Grant wasn't clubbing or out with other women, he was with his brother and that made him happy. That was all it was. It didn't mean he didn't love me or want to spend time with me like I had made up in my head. Of all people, I understood this. I chose to remain married and solve my own problems by not trying to change people when it's easier to just change myself.

Although, it took a lot of work and discipline to get there, I made the transition and became an asset, learned how to get along with the in-laws, handle myself and thrive into the expanding future. Proudly, I have earned every ounce of respect that others have granted me and I hold the respect and trust in high regard . I refuse to ever rest on my laurels.

Ironically, I have made myself such an asset, Grant only wants to spend time with me. He wants me everywhere and with him all the time. Now, with two kids and a husband to tend to as well as trying to accomplish all my personal goals, I long for alone time and often beg, *"Isn't there an Xbox game you can play?"*

The King: Unwavering, Committed, and Willing To Do Whatever It Takes

Ah, the king. The man in charge. The head honcho. The boss.

In my empire, Grant is all of those things, and more. There is no one higher within his businesses — and for good reason. He works harder than anyone in the entire kingdom, including me. He's ruthless, relentless, and has a standard of excellence that sets the bar high for others to do the same. He's our Triple Crown. The more he produces, the more we all flourish.

You might be king of your empire, or be married to, or dating your king. While the rules of each reign differ slightly, there are some absolutes that must be followed in order to succeed.

Poser Kings Need Not Apply

There are many, many people who claim they want to be the king (or pretend and act like they already are) but very few are willing to put in the work to earn their rightful crown. How many "kings" do we all see on social media driving cars they can't afford? Or wearing watches they charged to a credit card and throwing stacks of cash at the club while the rest of their lives are empty, broken and without money for the necessities?

The most powerful empires are built when the king is willing to sacrifice "pleasures" like these. He's willing to make the hard choices and envision the future so the empire expands and doesn't contract. He doesn't have a macho compulsion to impress his friends by overspending. He's intelligent with a knowledge he must build and multiply money and resources for long-term survival. Yet, he's also aware of his own shortcomings and is willing to learn, strengthen, and change in order to grow. He knows he must be confident, sharp and on top of the game. Low self-esteem can affect the kingdom in the form of an inflated ego, a false sense of pride, or a lack of confidence to pull the trigger on a really great opportunity.

Kings and queens while striving for greatness, learn from their mistakes. A king can't be both at the top of the throne and the joker at the same time. He must simultaneously think of himself, and of the good of the others who serve him and who he serves in return. In other words a king needs to not only walk his talk, he needs to create the path upon which he strides since he's the leader. Until then, skip the clubs and bottle service. Balling ain't cheap! And balling definitely isn't ballin' if you're a poser.

Kings Always Over Deliver

I've been with Grant for over fifteen years, and I've seen him work just as hard for a twenty-dollar sale as for a one-hundred-million dollar sale. That might sound crazy, but he has an incredible work ethic. He doesn't take for granted the value of hard work. He's willing to do the things he's not good at or hates to do in order to become a master of them.

Recently, we traded in our smaller plane for a brand new Gulfstream G550 that's equipped to fly us internationally. That was a huge deal for us — not just because of the price tag, but because taking the Cardone brand globally has been on our list of goals as a couple for several years. It's actually part of a much bigger goal that's two part:

one, to reach a global audience; and two, to reach a billion-dollar net worth.

The billionaire mindset is much different from the mindset of a millionaire. Every single move must be calculated with that figure in mind, all the while maintaining your existing empire. It's a lot of pressure, especially when it's your spouse (me) who suggested that you might want to become one in the first place. I can tell you Grant wasn't happy when I first brought it up.

One day out of the blue I mentioned rather emphatically, *"You need to become a billionaire!"* I hadn't really thought of how this would be perceived by a man who spends every waking moment trying to provide for me and his family, but it didn't go over well. Grant became furious at me. He was insulted. He accused me of not being satisfied with the abundances he had already provided for the family. He went on and on about how easy it was for me to sit back and set ridiculous, unattainable goals when he was the one pushing, shoving and grinding.

While he was ranting, I was calculating how to diffuse the situation. Don't think I wasn't tempted to say a few choice words myself, but I knew that would get me nowhere. So being the clever woman that I am, and willing to use every tool in my arsenal to get what I want, I decided to have sex with him. I knew this was the only solution that could possibly dismantle the bomb I had just dropped and it worked! Yes, ladies intimacy is an asset. It's OK to have sex with your husband. Use it wisely, and use it often.

Needless to say, in the afterglow, I was able to clarify what I meant. Grant is a giant and he needs to play big games. When a man of that magnitude plays at smaller levels, he gets bored with life and wants to devour everyone in sight. However, if he reached for a bigger target, it would be two-fold. Not only would he reach his goal of ending financial illiteracy by helping people on a global scale but also he would be forced to spend every moment focused on a massive target (other than me).

We would have to use every ounce of effort to destroy opposition and aid each other. When you are constantly reminded that you both are on the same team fighting a war, the war to win at life, you stop waging war on each other! There is no greater act of love you can give another than helping him or her achieve their goals. When you do that mutually, you create a love that truly becomes legendary.

The billion is a made up number. That's all it is. It is merely a symbol of reaching the masses, which is ultimately the goal. If you've made enough to money to have a billion dollars then you've probably have reached billions in order to do so. Look at the Forbes List. See who is on it and what their companies did to get there. They all have a common thread. They reached the masses.

My point was well-received the second time around. It helped launch a completely elevated side of Grant that I knew was waiting to come out. It also fortified us as a team. We aren't billionaires but at least now Grant believes he actually has a shot at it. For obvious reasons I haven't told him that the real target is being multi-billionaires and on the Forbes List. That will be our little secret for now. However, Grant has ALWAYS delivered what he has set out to do and has NEVER not delivered. He exceeds what was promised and has never let me down.

Grant is a beast in business, yet has always treated me with the utmost respect. He has earned my unshakable trust and devotion for life.

But kings, please know it's not always easy to be with a queen, especially when she's at your level. She'll be tougher on you than anyone you've ever met because she sees in you your full potential. We all have the ability to reach higher than our minds can imagine if we're willing to put that belief before action. In other words, know your "why" and figure out the "how" later. When it's earned, material things like money and jewelry are nice to have but at the end of the day they are just objects representative of a job well done. Even saying you're a king or a queen is pretty meaningless unless you've attached a purpose to it and are living by your value system accordingly.

Our billion-dollar moment will come one day. The day Grant walks into our home and announces that we've hit that target will be a very satisfying day indeed. You will have helped us with that and we will be always grateful to our fans.

Empire-Building Exercise: Write Out Your Role

Map out what your role is as king or queen of your empire. If you are in a relationship, list out who does what. You have to put the roles of "man/woman" aside and really come together as a unit to see who does what better. In our marriage, yes, the roles are a bit more traditional. I've seen many couples though with the breadwinner role reversed and the empire was equally successful because each knows their role. Yes, in a marriage you are equal but you are not equal in the roles that you both contribute to inside the marriage. Make an actual job description of what you do so if an area is booming or busting, you know who is responsible.

Grant understands business and runs five companies. This is not my strong suit and Grant dominates this field. He is the boss of the business — the income side of our relationship. I may offer opinions and advice but I understand he makes all the final decisions. It is his job to produce companies that are delivering and producing at extraordinary levels. Whatever decision he makes regarding the businesses, I trust it is the best and get behind it.

Similarly, we are not equals at home. The home, kids and behind-the-scenes operations are my areas of expertise. I run all these type of activities and make all executive decisions about anything pertaining to them. However, the same rules apply to him. He may offer suggestions and we will certainly discuss our children together but in the end, I make the final calls. The children and home environment are my products and I want my area flourishing and prospering to the best of my ability.

We understand in order to get to where we want to go, we have to assign posts or jobs to the one strongest suited for it. We don't compete with each other or fight each other trying to do the same role. There can only be one general. Two generals equal war. Delegate who is the general of what in your empire. Then, unite together and get busy producing the products of your job as the general of your department!

Chapter 4

The Lotto Game

Dead broke? Trapped in a "can't think bigger" mindset? Or, in general, salivating at the idea of a nine-figure windfall? Allow me to recommend the Lotto Game.

No Money — Mo' Problems

It was that horrible CRASH of 2008 when everything that could have gone bust in our lives did. The economic crash had just shaken the entire global economy and business slowed to a trickle.

So, what do you do when your back is against the wall and you're preparing for war? How about playing a game? In the most stressful of times, Grant and I always find a way to laugh and have fun. It's an underestimated tool that many overlook.

The Lotto Game

We called it the Lotto Game. The rules were pretty simple. You ask and answer a rhetorical question of what you would do if you won (after taxes) $200 million dollars. For a couple who were potentially about to meet their financial demise and hadn't yet figured out where to drum up even a fraction of that, it was a laughable concept. In truth, I wasn't laughing. Quite the opposite. I was terrified. Being the observant woman that I am, I knew Grant needed a break from the heaviness of it all. I decided to do what I do best. Have fun! I wanted to give him a sense of having something, rather than feeling everything was being taken away. I had to replace his self-doubt with getting him to feel powerful again. Trying to cuddle or give sympathy to a man of Grant's caliber was never going to work, so I got creative!

I asked Grant, *"What would you do if you won $200 million free and clear?"* He was reluctant to play the game and flipped the question on me. I said I would go on a global world tour and then find a way to spend the rest. I had a blast playing and it was the birth of my idea to take us on a global world tour. It would take ten years for this idea to manifest and become reality — but it did!

Grant, catching onto how the game worked and knowing before he spent any of this "money" he would need to find a way to multiply it. He would not just spend it. He said, *"I'd buy $150-million of multifamily real estate, pour a bit more into the other business and then maybe buy myself a watch."* He understood that money needs to multiply and not just be spent. He started to think in bigger and broader terms. After going back and forth a few rounds, we committed to playing the game every night for months as a way to keep ourselves motivated during the recession.

During that time, all of our spending except for anything that wasn't essential to staying alive had ground to an absolute stop. There was no free time spent loafing around. It was replaced with massive action! However, I loved the feeling of freedom and growth the Lotto Game gave us. We started to envision what it would really, truly feel like to have tangible financial freedom. We began to make the necessary changes in order to achieve that goal. We allowed ourselves to be people that felt free and became who we wanted to be without needing permission from some bank account statement.

I guarantee, if you play this game correctly and not just spending the money down to zero, you will operate on bigger and smarter levels. You will come to realize that you don't care about the material things when you have it all. You care about who you are and what your accomplishments and contribution to others will be. This game gave us permission to create what ultimately served as the blueprint for our legacy.

Mixed Emotions

Sometimes, playing the game made us sad. While we loved to play, comparing where we were to what our fantasy lives looked like felt like a stretch. We wanted it badly and we had to occasionally catch ourselves when anxiety set in. It might sound strange if you've never set out on a vision quest of your own but when you get a taste of what could be, even if it's just an idea, you begin to get hungry for it.

The Lotto game challenged my thinking. At first, it seemed like a huge sum but I slowly began to realize I wasn't reaching high enough. Why not push the Lotto Game to its limits, and think as big as possible? It became more about accumulating wealth in order to spend money on charities, people, and organizations that could benefit from our message.

Eventually, we pulled through. Grant made good on all the loans and we settled our lawsuit. We said goodbye to our beautiful home in California, with plans of rebuilding in Miami, Florida. We surpassed the $200 million target with plans to reach a billion. Who says fantasies can't come true?

Empire-Building Exercise: Play The Lotto Game

Whether you're in the midst of a personal financial crisis or sitting pretty cush, grab your spouse, your kids, or business partners and get started on a round of the Lotto Game. If you're rolling solo these days, get out a pad of paper and pen and play the game with yourself. Ask yourself what you would do with $200+ million. Pay attention to what you would spend your money on or what you would invest in. Then play the game again but each time increase the amount until you are finally a billionaire or multi-billionaire. Observe how you would feel knowing anyone would probably take your phone call once you were a multi-billionaire on the Forbes List. Get a good sense of what it really feels like to have the world at your fingertips. Do you have more confidence? Would you feel just a little bit more free to do and say what you want? Would you not take certain things too seriously anymore? Would you have less worry about money?

Now I want you to think about what are the difficult phone calls you need to make. Where have you avoided taking chances or risks for fear of failure? Who are the people you need to be in front of to expand your empire? Are you truly doing whatever it takes to get to the next level? What is a sum of money that seems entirely out of reach? What would you do with it if it was yours? Then assume the mindset that you already are a multi-billionaire and answer each of those questions with THAT viewpoint.

At the end of the day, the Lotto Game isn't just about fantasies and "what-ifs", it's about giving yourself permission to think as a king or a queen would. You deserve the freedom that massive thinking and financial independence can provide. Start with your mindset, and watch the action follow.

PART
THREE

Build Your Empire

"Whatever good things we build end up building us."
—Jim Rohn

Chapter 5

Get On The Same Page!

Getting on the same page as your partner is essential — there's no way around it. Yes, you can have a successful relationship if you're getting along, monogamous and keeping things status quo. It's only when you join forces though, that you'll truly make significant gains in your life and in business.

I like to reference Clydesdale horses. One Clydesdale can pull eight-thousand pounds alone. When two Clydesdales are harnessed side by side, the two horses can pull twenty-four-thousand pounds together totaling three times that of what they could do alone! Imagine if you and your partner were like Clydesdales? Imagine for a second the possibility of operating at three times your capacity.

Unfortunately, not all marriages or relationships consist of two Clydesdales or two Clydesdales pulling in the same direction. Two people can be physically present in the relationship but going in different directions, with different goals and aspirations, if any at all. Now imagine, trying to pull your eight-thousand pounds while your partner is pulling their eight-thousand pounds in the opposite direction. Do you get my point?

There is an immense power in having your partner 100% behind you — in your career, at home, and in your community. What feats could you accomplish, both independently and together? What roadblocks could you defeat? How big could your empire grow? Become that extra gust of wind that helps keep your partner motivated and focused at work, during a challenging time or simply to keep your relationship uplifted.

A Leap of Faith

Grant and I weren't always on the same page. Oh no. It took us getting over a few major roadblocks before I'd even consider marrying him. And I don't just mean the non-stop calls that took place for a year before we even went on a single date.

A couple of months after Grant proposed, he casually mentioned that he needed me to sign a prenuptial agreement. I was shocked, devastated and felt heartsick because even though I may have been a lot of other things, I wasn't a quitter. I knew this relationship had the makings to be something great but I told him I wouldn't marry him if he needed me to sign a prenup. I am a ride-or-die chick. I may have been severely messed up when it came to love and relationships but if I commit to something I'll die fighting rather than quit. And I certainly wasn't going to start this marriage on opposite pages!

"If you think I'm marrying you for your money, you would be marrying the wrong girl and you have no clue of what I am made." I was twenty-nine at this time. I simply stated, *"I have never been married because I would rather be single my whole life then quit on something. If I get married, I'm in for life. Divorce is not an option. If you need an out, then I'm not the one."*

Grant looked at me, stunned. He wasn't, and still isn't used to hearing "no." Especially when a prenup is a logical, protectionary component of many marriages. Not ours, though. I gave Grant a simple choice. He could have my heart, and an "I do", or we part ways with no hard feelings.

In 2004, at thirty years old and on the Fourth of July, we got married with no prenuptial. Just us, and our commitment to each other and to the future. But this was only the first of several hurdles we would have to overcome in our journey of married life together. Getting back and remaining on the same page as quickly as possible when things go awry will keep you operating at optimum levels together.

Trust Takes (More) Time

At first, married life wasn't that much different than our dating life. We lived and spent time together. Dined together. Went to parties and events together. Enjoyed monogamy. Asked each other about our days etc. I don't know if I'd call us true teammates at that point but marriage doesn't come with an instruction manual. You sort of just figure it out as you go.

Still, there was a part of me that was deeply, if secretly, concerned about my own survival. There was the girl, Elena Lyons, and worse "Lane Rose", who lived deep inside of the now Mrs. Grant Cardone and they had learned to trust no one and to get by on their own. My parents ingrained in me from a young age that I could never depend on a man. Even if I got married, I should make sure to have my own life and count my own successes.

So, that's what I did. Aside from the normal couple activity I just described above, I soldiered on in my career. Even though Grant gave me no reason to doubt him, and hello, I'd just made a huge deal about not signing a prenup, I felt like I had to have a backup plan in case he ever screwed me over. For the first four years of our marriage, I never fully relaxed into being Grant's wife. Getting on the same page may require a little bit of time and an ounce of effort. In the meantime, Grant continued to prove himself as an honorable, trustworthy, unshakable man who would go to ends of the world for me.

The Great Wakeup

Sometimes, you leap out of your comfort zone. Other times, the universe shakes you out. For better or for worse, it was the 2008 recession, that like many of you, rattled us to the core.

I'll never forget sitting on our sofa in our beautiful living room on top of the Hollywood Hills. The news was on, and Lehman Brothers had just filed bankruptcy. I was pregnant with our first child, and as I looked toward Grant for reassurance, a terrified expression took over his face. *"What does this mean?"* I asked, rubbing my expanding belly. Grant turned to me, and point blank said, *"It means we're going to die!"*

I actually thought he was joking at first. I quickly figured out that this was no joke and my heart sank to the pit of my soul. I was angry — fuming, furiously mad. A real man doesn't let his wife and unborn child "die" because of an economic collapse! I turned to Grant, sharply pointed to my stomach, and said, *"We won't die! I don't die! Do we look like death to you? Now go to your office, and do NOT come out until you figure this out!"*

I knew that action, and not sitting around waiting for the news to update with continued doom and gloom was going to get us to whatever next step we needed to take.

Three-hours later Grant marched out of his office, weary but focused with a thick printout under his arm. It was the manuscript for his first book, now known as Sell Or Be Sold. As he handed it to me, he apologized, *"This my first book. It won't make us rich but I now know exactly what I have to do. And, Elena, I promise to never scare you again."*

And he kept his word.

Nothing Ventured, Nothing Gained

At this point, my own gig was up. There was no more time to care about only myself and my personal solvency. I had to put everything on the line and go all in, not just on our marriage, but on Grant. The business of being married to an entrepreneur in one of the most trying financial times in history was officially my new full-time job. I committed and it was full-steam ahead.

After twenty years in the entertainment business, it was time to give up my acting career in order to have Grant's back. Believe me when I say it wasn't an easy decision. It's also not easy to tell your friends and family that you, as a woman, are going all-in on your man. Especially in a culture that advises women to be wary of men, and that women and wives are replaceable.

Bold moves are the only kind that pay. Acting was something I could always come back to. Taking the reins of what ultimately proved to be one of our biggest opportunities in expanding the business was not. This was officially the moment Grant and I got on the same page. And it's where we've remained ever since.

Opinions Don't Pay The Bills

Grant's plan included a way to reach masses of potential customers, readers and viewers. This group would not be just within the automotive and sales training industries in which he was known, but to all. He would expand his own brand of recognition to everyone and not just to one niche group. Grant's needs became my number-one concern. Anything he needed from me, I did. I didn't complain or nag if he had to work late or travel. This was a team effort. I knew in order to be a truly powerful couple, I had to nix the naysayers and their opinions of Grant having me wrapped around his little finger and that I was losing my own identity. I won't lie, I did secretly feel like this from time to time.

However, there was no time to care about what anyone thought. At the end of the day, opinions don't pay the bills — and when you aim to build an empire, they only distract you from your purpose.

Piece by piece, we began to shed our old life and rebuild a new one. Over time, as Grant's business grew, so did our empire and the realization that our experience would one day help and inspire other couples to get through their own challenges. It took us ten years, a cross-country move, and a hell of a lot of sacrifices, but I can now say with pride that we're finally financially free. I've never once regretted paying my own personal price of leaving behind a career that at one point was a huge part of who I thought I was.

Sell Or Be Sold

The question I am asked the most is, *"What do I need to do to get my partner/spouse on the same page?"*

The answer is simple. Become the best salesperson you know. You've got to sell your partner on the vision of your future together. Find out each other's purposes or what would motivate them to become a true teammate and appeal to that.

For example, if the wife's vision is she wants the kids to have a college fund, set one up and make small contributions so she can see that it's real. It's easier for a partner to support one another when there is a focused reason with actual systems in place that have targets and goals. You also need to SEE when you are hitting targets and experience victories together. This is what continues to bond you as a couple. Find a way to start turning these dreams into realities. Get those pie-in-the-sky ideas out of your head by setting something up in the physical universe. Take actions that make it real even if it will be years before the final goal has been attained. I'm about to sound like Yoda here because this is so simple, but here goes, *"When you make it real, it becomes real."*

Something real can be backed with trust. You don't have to cross your fingers and have blind faith in some fantasy when reality is staring you in the face. When you finally find that purpose you both are passionate about, you will become Special Forces teammates with the unwavering drive to crush every mission together. Playing at a higher level requires a commitment, not just to each other, but to a greater cause — your empire.

It also means you are each pulling your weight — remember the Clydesdales. You've got to operate and perform in good times, in bad times, and especially during shit-hits-the-fan times. Grant and I remain solid on this one fact: we do not bring 50/50 to the table while others may. We each bring 100/100 at all times. Because we are not Clydesdales, I'm convinced together we pull far more than only three times our weight. I'm thinking at least 10X!

When you start operating and winning as a couple on the same page, you develop a deeper sense of pride in each other. As you continue achieving your goals, you'll find yourself cheering him or her on. A win for one is a win for all. Wins create and establish long-term love.

From watching other people's relationships, the most important lesson I have observed is if you let your partner quit on their dreams, soon enough, they'll quit on everything else — including you. As the saying goes, *"The way you do one thing is the way you do everything."* I have seen far too many partners that try to stop the other from chasing their dreams. It could be out of fear, jealousy, or other insecurities that the partner will leave if they succeed. It always ends the same. The one who was forced to quit will ALWAYS quit in the end.

If this sounds like you, figure out a way to handle yourself. I say this all the time, *"Find the one you trust and build an empire."* If you don't trust your partner, maybe pick a different partner. But, one day you will have to trust in order to let each other grow to your maximum potential. It will only make them love you even more.

Empire-Building Exercise:
Get Clear On Your Status As a Couple
(a.k.a. Get On The Same Page)

Moment of truth, empire-builders, are you willing to go all-in on your relationship?

I don't mean to go ahead and get married before you're ready. Or quit your job, or engage in any other extreme measure for the sake of acting out or trying to be at a place where you are not. Rather, check yourself, where in your relationship have you held back, or poured more into yourself than your collective unit?

First, get a pad of paper and create three columns. In the left column write down your goals. In the middle column write down your goals as a couple. Finally, in the right column write down your partner's goals.

For example, Grant and I strive to serve as a model couple, be the best parents, donate to our church as well as various charities, and reach all seven billion people in the world. These are a few of the goals that go into our middle column.

I strive to be a great wife, mom, an empire builder who wants to help other empire builders make their lives and relationships better, philanthropist, shooter, and martial arts student. Those go in my left column.

Grant strives to be a successful businessman, husband, father and wants to help entrepreneurs around the world to be able to provide for their families. That goes in the right column.

Both your columns of personal goals should feed your middle column and ultimately make your middle column better for it. The end columns are there to support and flow power to your middle column and should in no way be acting as a liability to the relationship.

If you find that one column is particularly heavy, or that you're lacking any goals as a couple, this is a chance for you to work together to figure out what it is you want to accomplish, and what your empire represents. Maybe you've found that over time, your couple goals have slid by the wayside and that in hindsight, you haven't been hitting your targets as well as you'd have liked. Recommit and make the decision to get on the same page.

Grant and I meet every Sunday to talk about our goals and where we are going. It helps to keep us on the same page and recommit weekly to the journey ahead. If you find yourself feeling resentful over any imbalances on your goal lists, start a conversation with your partner. Remember you're either creating or destroying your empire so use this as a way to get on the same page — not off. We all know too well, life punishes the unprepared. Taking stock of your capabilities as a couple will help you weather any storm. Extraordinary relationships, like extraordinary lives, are made, not given.

Chapter 6

Seek Your Own Counsel

Grant and I are all about using the power of social media as a way to build and strengthen our empire. We love to connect with people and there's genuinely no better feeling than to get a message of *"Thanks"* from someone whose life has been changed from the content we put out.

But there's something you'll never see in our feeds or outside our home — the private, intimate details of our marriage and family life. Those are sacred including the inevitable rough spots that occur in every relationship. Those belong to us — and only us.

Oversharing Can and Will Cost You

We live in a strange new world where airing your dirty laundry is no longer shameful, and instead, encouraged. It doesn't matter if it's on Facebook or amongst your circle of friends while out to brunch, somehow it's become okay to share with people, often strangers, the issues you have at work or in your marriage. I can tell you, this is not only a horrible idea and practice, but will create bigger problems much tougher to spring back from.

For instance, once you have settled the disagreement you and your partner were having, the "bad press" you created still exists with your friends and family. It can completely sabotage you. You have just convinced others how bad your partner is. Later, when your friends are whispering about it to each other, and making comments to you about how awful you have it, it can rekindle that flame of fury. You can find yourself constantly upset about an argument long since settled out.

It is vital to keep your marriage sacred for you and your spouse. When you not only respect the other person, you build more trust making you both fortified allies through thick and thin. Knowing you have someone who will protect and defend you in life, will make you invincible. Your well-intentioned parents, in-laws, best friends and therapists are not seated alongside your throne. So why would you defer your problems to them? When you could, and should, work them out with your spouse. Make it your policy not to engage in conversation about your home life with other people as a means of seeking comfort, or to have your concerns validated.

Trust me, there was a time in my life when it felt comfortable to turn to my girlfriends to complain about whatever drama was happening. These open-ended venting sessions shared equally among us had no real solutions in sight except to pour another glass of wine. Just as Twitter is only a click away, so is the ability to visit with a therapist and get a prescription that will supposedly and magically cure all of your problems. What do these outlets have in common? They're cheap, easy, and disposable — all of the things an empire are not.

The Answers Are Within You

So who do you turn to when the chips are down and things are horrible in your relationship? It might seem counterintuitive but the answer is your partner. Seek your own counsel — in each other.

This means a few things. FIRST: You need to work on the communication within your relationship to ensure that your needs are being met. Which in turns lessens the temptation to seek outside opinion or advice and forces you to rely on your own strengths to work through whatever issue is on the table. If this is a weak area for you, commit the energy needed to work on it.

Practice letting someone finish what they are saying in entirety before you cut them off and try to defend yourself as well as redirect the blame. Sometimes you both just need to hear each other out and that alone diffuses the matter. Although you may not always get your partner to see your side or do what you want, you have to be willing to allow your partner to have their reality in the situation. Often times, it's not about you trying to get them to change. It's about you figuring out how YOU can deal with the situation going forward. Unfortunately, the secret lies in you having to change by finding your own solution. You will absolutely exhaust yourself and drive yourself insane trying to change someone who is completely against it. Of course, I am strictly talking about non-damaging type situations that are more annoying than destroying. Certainly, you have to come to a resolution on detrimental problems if someone is acting in a way to destroy the non-negotiables of the relationship.

Get over the Blame Game!

Whenever I find myself being really irritated with Grant and times are getting really tough the first thing I do is take responsibility for what I'm doing that is contributing to the problem. Once I straighten this out I feel better again. Magically, I am not blaming Grant anymore and I can have a rational conversation with him about whatever topic needs to be addressed.

Once we have handled the subject but it continues to be a problem, I immediately know someone or something has infiltrated the empire. Someone is in our environment and is either knowingly or unknowingly causing problems. You have to find out who has a negative outlook about some aspect of your relationship or who is talking in your ear about it. Again, you are responsible for listening, so knock it off.

The issue could be something silly and simple. Several years back, Grant and I were fighting about ridiculous things for no apparent reason. We had started watching Real Housewives of Beverly Hills and all of the characters on that show have very dysfunctional relationships. Grant was agitated because he felt several of the women seemed materialistic and acted like they were entitled to a certain lifestyle that perhaps they hadn't earned. At this same time we started having some really bizarre arguments. We finally identified the source of our arguments as the show and agreed to never watch it again. Immediately our fights ceased.

You are responsible for letting people or even the TV media (who apparently love to promote the destruction of relationships and marriages) into your life. Look, I'm from the Hollywood world and I can tell you all shows are scripted. Don't kid yourself. People have been placed in scenarios, storylines have been edited, all to fit a narrative that creates enough controversy to shock and capture your attention. The networks then sell your captured attention to advertisers and make money. Unfortunately, with enough bad information hitting you from all angles, it becomes mainstream thinking. This will take a toll on your relationship if you aren't aware enough to recognize these outside influences and their potential to affect you.

SECOND: You need to exercise emotional discipline when you're around your friends and family. That doesn't mean you need to ditch them, act like a robot or pretend that your life is perfect. But to assume that someone outside of your relationship knows what's best for it, is a mistake. Abusive relationships are not included in this category. By all means, if you find that you're in a dangerous situation, please get help and get out.

THIRD: There is an exception here, and that is seeking the guidance from a spiritual counselor, such as a member of your church. Note, I said guidance, not advice. You want someone who can maintain a neutral position and doesn't have an ulterior motive to influence you one way or another. If you're not religious skip this step or apply this principle to another civic-minded leader within your own personal empire whom you trust.

And, please don't get into the habit of collecting counseling the way you would pick up business cards at a networking event. It's toxic and you might as well be back at happy hour, mixing two-for-one drink specials with your spouse's latest transgressions.

Set The Bar

No one would dare talk badly about Grant in front of me and the same is true for anyone who would think about bad-mouthing me in front of him. It's not a scare tactic. The person who dared would receive quite an earful to say the least! Even when we're working out issues behind the scenes, rest assured, we will always come to the other's defense no matter what. When you have enough integrity for your relationship, you inspire other people to do the same. Over time, you'll notice that everyone within your empire follows the same set of standards and that the whiners and complainers have slowly but surely faded from sight. Positivity begets more positivity.

On the flip side, I don't know of a single person who has a perfect marriage — certainly not mine. The flaws of a relationship are what make it unique and just as no two people are alike, neither are any two relationships. Playing the comparison game can be very destructive to your empire. In fact, it's worse, because it can lead to "what if" fantasies when the reality is you probably have a great relationship that just needs a bit of attention.

Empire-Building Exercise: Create Your Counsel

Make a list of everyone you've typically gone to when you've had an argument or upset with your partner. If needed, go through your recent texts and call history to see if there are any instances where a quick check-in has evolved into a vent-fest.

Next, look over your list, and ask yourself objectively how does it feel to know that your partner isn't there to defend him or herself when you complain about your relationship? Probably not very good. That's why confronting our issues head-on is the only surefire way to nip bad behavior in the bud and change our habits.

Right here, right now, decide do you want to continue to build your empire or not? If the answer is yes, make the commitment not only to your relationship, but to yourself. Stop the gossiping, complaining, and advice-seeking sessions.

To support your decision, roleplay. Write out what you'll say the next time someone asks how things are going with your partner or spouse. If your tendency is to say something negative, write down five things you like or love about your partner. It'll help you focus on the positive. My go-to is, *"We aren't perfect, but we have a good thing going."* It tends to put negative people right in their place and shuts the conversation down quickly. Some others are, *"We are a good team. We have each other's back."* Your one-liners might feel strange at first, even fake, but eventually it'll feel like second nature. Taking a pause before you answer and drawing your higher purpose to mind can help.

Going forward, and there's no way around this, you've got to resist the temptation to participate in group partner-bashing. Or you need to find a new group to hang out with, period. You can't build an empire if you're going to jump off a bridge just because everyone else is doing it.

Now, look and see if you are being negatively influenced by TV, media, social media, etc. Have the discipline to eliminate those specific influences if they are affecting you. If you happen to be in the "what if" category and are using social media or other forms of entertainment to fantasize about others while thinking you are on the same page as your partner, you are fooling yourself. You are either creating or destroying. And that would certainly count as destroying. The more you look at others, the more you will see wrong with your partner. Remember, you are trying to build an empire. It requires trust and that requires discipline in order to do the right thing. Stop driving yourself mad over the "what if" and focus that attention back into creating your own relationship.

Chapter 7
Say 'No' To Normal

Come around the Cardone household, and you'll quickly learn that "normal" is a four-letter word best checked at the door.

Normal, or average, is a way of thinking that keeps many people cemented in place, in jobs, careers, relationships, places, and habits that get them by but never get them ahead. It's an acceptance of the status quo, and finding comfort in what's easy and readily available instead of a stretch and a reach. Normal is being contented with average levels of action and never striving to push for greater levels of anything. It is being OK with what life gives you rather than staking a claim on what could be yours. It's vital that you realize that normal will MAYBE get you a house with a white picket fence, but it'll never build an empire.

Normal Marriages Are Toxic

"Normal" is keeping up with the status quo, boxing yourself in and ticking off a checklist of what is or isn't right. It's coasting on automatic so that you'll always fit in and always say and appear to do the right things — ultimately convincing yourself that you are normal and everything is just fine. Unfortunately, normal can only last for so long.

Normal is the most dangerous state to be in because of those factors alone. You THINK everything is ok until it's not. Bad things happen to good people every day. Normal is not strong or tough enough to withstand the impact of life's major blows. No one plans on someone in the family getting sick or injured, lawsuits, a death, an economic collapse, getting laid off, a natural disaster, or what I see most commonly, a husband or wife who cheats while the stunned partner thought everything was "good." Normal is a delusional and treacherous state that I often warn against.

Normal marriages are destroyed as soon as some hot piece of tail comes along. All the sudden, the guy or girl's heart skips a beat and then starts wondering "what if?" What's really happening is they're thinking that somehow this will be an above average deal. They are looking to escape those normal, monotonous, mundane sensations also known as "mediocrity" that flows through their veins.

Only extraordinary marriages are strong enough to look temptation in the face and say, "pass." Even in extraordinary marriages, the right decisions are hard to resist at times. However, when the "what if" option is met with a "stay with extraordinary" or "hope for halfway special", the choice is always an easy one in the end.

Extraordinary has built up reserves of honor, trust, love, hotness, sexiness, passion, ride or die, support, fun, laughter, sex, energy, life, beauty, health, adventure, and the list can go on. Even in the worst of fights, the thought of losing the extraordinary is so devastating that the thought of adultery actually becomes repulsive. If you can't imagine the thought of adultery being repulsive, rest assured you have never been in anything close to an extraordinary relationship.

However, for the sake of this book, and because I hear some of you asking that burning question, *"What would you do if Grant cheated on you?"* I'll respond.

You might think I'm crazy for saying this, but after the anger settled, I would honestly have to look at how I contributed to this unwanted situation. What did I do or not do that made him want to do that? How did I become normal and deliver a subpar marriage? Where did

I get too comfortable and not deliver? How did I let him down? Was it continuously over a long period of time or an isolated incident?

I can hear all my ladies screaming now, so let me clarify. I am NOT saying that this behavior is acceptable or tolerable nor am I saying it would all be my fault. I'm definitely not a pushover wife that thinks she unworthy, her husband can do no wrong, and I'm to blame for everything. I don't have that syndrome where I think I deserved it.

On the flip side of this, if I ever cheated, I'd also look at what I did that made me betray him like that. No matter what side of the equation I was on, the cheater or the cheated on, I'd take responsibility for whatever aspect of it I could and do whatever it took to mend the damage. Obviously, the cheating party would have more damage to mend. Full disclosure would be a requirement as true trust and love cannot be built on a bed of secrets. I would analyze what the circumstances were to determine if we wanted to continue the union or dissolve the nuptials.

If we both decided to remain together, it would mean being willing to leave the past in the past, commit to rebuilding, and earning our way back to greatness. Fortunately, Grant has never placed me in this scenario. I have worked extremely hard in life, and in my marriage to be above average. I know I am Grant's greatest asset. I don't say that out of arrogance but I do say it assertively and with confidence. I am Grant's greatest asset.

Hopefully, I have done a good enough job at making him realize the thought of losing me would be more painful than he could tolerate. However, after fifteen years, I refuse to rest on my laurels and fight every day in the pursuit of greatness in myself and in my marriage.

Cheating is just one example of how a marriage fails.

When spouses become cold and unwilling to communicate, that's a failed marriage. When a marriage is lifeless and sexless, no matter how many years on paper you've been together, that's a failed marriage. A divorce, clearly, is a sign of a destroyed marriage. And yet if you take a look around, you can see that it's become socially acceptable to acknowledge these flaws as the ticket to freedom of modern life rather than putting in the work to step it up on all levels.

Fans of the G&E (Grant and Elena) Show know how passionate I am about the benefits of being married to the right person and bringing your all to your partner. Marriage has been a game changer in so many ways, and I'm not just talking about the financial side effects of marrying a successful man. Grant and I could be completely penniless, yet because our mindset is right and geared toward growth, we'll always be rich — and that "broke" state would be temporary at best.

Work On Yourself First. It's your First Line of Defense

It's so easy to find flaws in other people that we often don't know we have them ourselves. I'm not talking about the external stuff. How many times do we look and challenge what we see internally? Are you so set in your ways that you already think you know best on just about everything? Are you willing to look at adjusting a few things that could make a huge impact on your life?

It's far more important to work on yourself from the inside out. You can be the most show-stopping woman (or man) in the room, but if you're a pretty package with a bunch of internal chaos, it won't be long before the glitzy paper, bells, and whistles fall off and that broken interior is exposed.

The twenty-two years I was working as an actress in Hollywood taught me that you've got to have a rock-solid handle on who you are in order to survive, never mind thrive. It's a cutthroat industry that will pick apart aspects of yourself you didn't even know existed. I can't even count the number of drop-dead, gorgeous, talented woman I watched get picked apart and crushed. These flaw pickers did it as a means to manipulate these girls to make them feel small, insecure and even needy. It's the way these people try to control women to keep them under lock and key.

The sad thing is, none of what these men said was even true. But these poor girls would do just about anything to fix the problem, even if it was harmful to themselves. They would starve themselves, take any fat-burning/appetite suppressing drugs they could get their hands on, throw up after a meal, undergo plastic surgery, lose all sense of themselves, and even sleep with these rat bastards. If you didn't have a good moral compass, you were chewed up and spit out! This industry doesn't just target women, by the way, men are targeted as well. However it's not at the forefront of conversation yet, and many men refuse to talk about it. But I can tell you first hand, I've seen it all.

I'd rather you have a good assessment of yourself and an accurate inventory of your strengths and weakness. This will help you differentiate between these awful creatures and a good guy just giving a positive, much-needed critique. From all my years of observing people and life, which I do A LOT of, here's a little hint, and probably not what you would expect. The people who want to manipulate you will attack your strengths not your weakness.

You might assume someone would attack your weaknesses but I find this seldom is the case. That is why it's vital you really have an accurate assessment of both. The evil people of the world will attack your strengths first. It's the equivalent of going straight for the jugular. Whatever you think is your strongest suit, is what is going to get attacked. They will start "flaw-picking" in that area. They try to confuse you and make you self-doubt your strengths knowing you have nothing to fall back on. Certainly, your weaknesses can't support you. If they attacked your weaknesses like most think they do, you always have your strengths to carry you through, so the damage is minimal.

The vultures weaken you by throwing you off your game. You become vulnerable when your strong suit or armor is weakened. It can't protect you if it's damaged. Once they knock you from your power then your weaknesses only magnify until you fully break. Now they start feeding into your weaknesses. If your weaknesses are drugs, alcohol, gambling, or strip clubs, rest assured you will be placed in those environments and encouraged to partake. You will implode on yourself and never see that your best friend was truly your worst enemy.

If your weaknesses are that you don't want to confront people, believe the best of them, or are too sensitive, this is what they will use. After they have completely introverted you on all your strengths, they'll use that you won't confront them in order to rob you blind, or steal your job, your husband, your wife or your business. Knowing you would never suspect them because you "believe the best of people," they would play to your sensitivity (your weakness) and make you feel sorry for them that their cat died, their car broke down or that they are getting evicted and have two kids or whatever other sob story they drum up to render them "harmless." All the while, secretly happy watching you go down in flames. Your demise actually brings them inner joy but on the surface, they will say things like, *"I'm only trying to help"* or *"I want what's best for you."* These people are severely hard to detect but you must be willing to see that not all people have good intentions like you do.

This is why I never leave home without being armored up. I used to be so naive and not know that I was. The second chances I gave trying to help these poor "innocent" people because I was so "nice" and felt so sorry for them. I caught a friend who had stolen two-thousand dollars from me and gave her a second chance. Six months later, after she had proved to be a reliable good friend again, I loaned her sixty-thousand dollars to pay off all her credit card loans. I wanted to help solve her problems and have her have a fresh start with a clean slate. After all, she was a longtime friend who I believed wanted to be better and I was determined to help. We worked out her payment plan and were good to go until she up and left. She changed all her contact information and never paid back a cent.

Unfortunately, I am embarrassed to say this wasn't the only incident where the wool was pulled over my "sweet" little eyes. There were dozens and dozens of these types of occurrences until I honed in on all my strengths and weakness. It wasn't until I was willing to see what was in front of me and confront that people actually intended to harm me, that I was able to vastly turn my life and our empire around.

Now, I know I'm naive and that goes into my weakness category so I always have to ask myself, *"Am I being naive here?"* and that usually guides me to the right answer. I never let my radar down even if I let you think I did. I am continually reading and assessing everyone at all times through all my strengths and weaknesses filters. It doesn't shut off. This isn't a curse, it's actually one of my most valuable strengths. It has saved us countless times from getting "in bed" with the wrong people. We have avoided many catastrophes and harmful situations because of this ability alone.

Just as it is important to know who is against you, you must also recognize who really is for you. The people with good intentions who want to help you, actively support you. These people will build up your strengths by helping you become more powerful and steer you away from your weaknesses. They aren't always nice and sweet. Sometimes, they are ferocious and want to push you to become better. They may appear to be "flaw pickers" but they are not! Make sure you recognize the difference between these two types of people. Often times, these people are tough and they push you to push yourself. You might be tempted to get angry with these people. However, if you know who is pushing you to greatness rather than pushing you into the ground, you will be better for it! You don't want to mistakenly kill off your most valuable teammates just because your feelings got hurt when ultimately, they were truly helping you in the process.

To this day, I diligently work on myself strengthening weaknesses and building strengths. The work is never done in this game called life. And just like in the game of chess, I'd rather be a grandmaster then a mere little pawn.

"Love Them The Way They Are" Is Total BS

I'm going to share with you another unpopular opinion. Your husband or wife doesn't want the cheaper, second-hand version of you.

Yes, doing the work on yourself means channeling inward and battling demons so that you're better equipped to deal with the day-to-day in your role as queen or king. But I won't lie, my decision to workout, eat healthy and take care of myself also has to do with the fact that it's what I brought to the table when I first met Grant over fifteen years ago. I enjoy being that sexy, smart, passionate partner that Grant couldn't live without when we were dating. It's a gift I bring to our marriage, just as he does the same for me.

Society has conditioned us to believe that we should just love and accept the people in our lives for who they are. Even when they get sloppy and let us down. It's a way of tugging at our heartstrings and decrying us as superficial if we're honest and say, *"I'm sorry, but I'm not attracted to you with those twenty-five extra pounds."* Of course, you will still love them but the attraction is different.

Marriage and love, just like an empire, are created and destroyed daily. We can fantasize all we want about an ideal scenario — spouses who never check out other people in restaurant corners, husbands or wives who don't cheat or your spouse being eternally in love and only having eyes for you. But not putting in the effort over long periods of time falls into the destruction category. Your husband or wife married you to have a true partner in life, not a roommate who's given up on themselves. It's a hard pill to swallow, I know. No one wants to talk about or mention it. But for the sake of getting you in top-notch shape (literally) to rule your empire, I will.

When you give up on yourself, you also give up on your partner. The more you feel bad about yourself, lose confidence or become self-conscious, your attention no longer flows outward on your spouse or on the other things you are creating. Instead, that attention flows inward onto you, focusing on how you feel about your body affecting you in a negative way. Over time, you find that you are irritable toward your partner over simple things and withdraw yourself physically from them. But if you really look at it, you are not feeling at your best physically or mentally and you end up taking it out on them.

The same is true for one's mental health and state of mind. No one wants to be with a hot wife or husband who can't keep their issues in check and wind up flooding the relationship. Work on yourself to not only physically make yourself feel in great shape but also because it's vital to keep that attention off of yourself. Keep your attention outward, on others, and on your projects. You will hit your targets faster and easier when you aren't consumed by loathing yourself to death.

Chapter 8

Sweat The Small Stuff

If you've never heard this story before, brace yourself. For you women who have my back, you might be tempted to toss this book across the room.

Several months after I had my second baby I was in a rut. The kind where brushing your hair is optional and you get into the groove of wearing sweatpants each and every single day. I couldn't seem to pull myself together beyond the scope of just existing and making those last ten additional pounds I kept post-pregnancy even more comfortable.

Grant, ever the kind-hearted soul, took notice of my new fashion sense, or lack thereof, and the few extra pounds I was carrying around and decided to mention it one day while we were in the kitchen. (How fitting!)

"What's with those same sweats you wear every day?" Grant said.

"They're comfortable! What's it to you?" I replied in quite an annoyed tone.

"You look like you have to lose a few..." he said, pausing as I whirled around, my eyes locked onto his eyes in a grip of death. Ladies, you know the kind of look I'm talking about.

"What," I seethed, *"I need to lose a few what?"*

"...Leaves," he stuttered, slowly taking a step back from the counter.

[Silence]

"Leaves? Leaves? I need to lose a few leaves?" I questioned.

What he really meant to say was pounds. Which in some marriages, might have resulted in Grant sleeping either on the couch or outside for a few weeks, if not the rest of his life.

At Casa de Cardone, however, the rules are a little different. We hold each other to a higher standard.

While my weight and how I look were, and are, not typically part of the conversation, my lackluster attitude about life was showing up all over the place, including my normally slim waistline. Rather than run off and seek sympathy in my "oh so supportive" friends which I was tempted to do, I had the courage to confront the situation instead. Grant in his awfully clumsy way was trying to tell me I got comfortable. As much as I did NOT want to workout and eat right, that is what I did. As a result, I felt myself come back to life little by little. I truly believe that fitness is a very important cure-all for those who need a boost in the happiness or health department.

Leaves though... You can believe me when I tell you he's never brought up the word again.

The Big Picture Starts With The Small Stuff

Of course, this isn't about "leaves," sweatpants, or about "just wanting a guy who loves me for who I am, no matter what." It's about taking care of the small things first so that I can set myself up for some big wins. I don't mean you have to dress to perfection every time you walk outside your house or spend hours primping. But little movements in the right direction are extremely beneficial.

When my life feels stuck, in a lull, out of control or just plain frustrating, that's when I put in the extra effort to get myself moving. This is not the time to withdraw from the world on the couch with a bucket of ice cream. Instead, I'll force myself to go workout. I'll eat extra healthy, avoid the sugar and drink more water. Then I make sure to get out of that workout gear. I can't stay in it all day. I'll get into a cute outfit that makes me feel good and apply a dash of makeup. I always feel better. Literally just moving your body from one activity to the next is helpful. It focuses your mind on other things and off of the troubling thoughts that are consuming your mind.

If I am still not out of my funk, I put my attention outward and focus on small tasks like making my bed, decluttering a closet or completing a long overdue house or office project. I just need a sense of accomplishment, no matter how trivial it might seem in the scheme of things. It's crucial for you to find ways to get yourself out of your slump, depression or whatever people call it these days. It is not up to your friends or your partner to fill that void or fix your mind. They can help you, support you, stand by your side but it is YOU that has to do the work and get yourself lifted. Just do the work. You don't need to pop a pill that artificially numbs you, inspires you, makes you happy or gives you a false sense of self-worth. Just muster up a little energy to get yourself going. Get into action. Surround yourself with like-minded people who push you. Drop the deadbeats and go chase your passions.

It can be easy to wallow in negative feelings. Everyone has a bad day once in a while. When those thoughts become pervasive, however, they become a part of your life and unfortunately, that dark corner will dominate to the point where it can destroy your empire.

Get out of your own way, and get on with it.

Never Say "NO!" - To Sex

If you chose to live an extraordinary life, odds are, you're going to want an extraordinary mate. Just as I reject a normal way of being, so does Grant. In a way, we feed off of each other. We are always pushing and supporting the other to become better and that's what shows up in our marriage. Sometimes we can be tough on one another in the process but one thing will always remain.

I married the man I love. I don't deny him anything he wants or needs — yep, that includes intimacy. We have a monogamous relationship, meaning we only have sex with each other. I could not tolerate if he didn't want to be with me intimately. He is the only one who I share that part of my life with. Yes, I married my best friend as well but I didn't just marry my best friend. I want to have sex with my lover, my spouse, and he wants that as well.

I would never reject the person I love the most. He experiences so much rejection in the outside world that I would never want to bring a sliver of that into our home life or bedroom. I want to build him up, love him, care for him, patch up all his wounds and send him back out to battle with the confidence of his woman beside him.

As his wife and lover, in fifteen years, he has never been told, *"No,"* *"I have a headache,"* or *"Not tonight."* I might not be able to save him from all the rejections and no's of the world but he will never hear it from me.

Empire-Building Exercise 1:
Get Comfortable Getting Uncomfortable

First, know that starting the work on yourself isn't going to be convenient. There will never be a window of time that opens up just for you, where everything in life is calm, pleasant, happy, and you're able to just burrow away and do all sorts of self-improvement exercises as you please. You have to carve out the time and make it a priority.

I say this because I don't want you to make excuses for why you have or haven't started this exercise in a week, a month, or a year from now. If you find yourself reading all sorts of self-help books but not applying what you are learning, you're avoiding by putting a barrier between you and the actual things you need to be doing. Stop avoiding and start confronting.

With that said, I want you to practice getting uncomfortable, or as my military friends say, *"Get comfortable being uncomfortable."* It starts with examining areas that you've accepted as normal. Look at your marriage, child rearing, your career, your health, your appearance, take a pick. If it helps, make a list. Examine the list. Get real about where you are this very minute. Then, take one item on the list and pick one thing you can do today, and do it. Start getting in the habit of doing things. Get ideas out of your head and DO them in the physical universe. The thoughts and ideas you get are your genius and your creativity calling on you. It's that inner voice guiding you to your greatness. Don't wait weeks or months until finally the thought vanishes from sight. When you get in the habit of ignoring that "genius" within, it stops coming to you.

The way to get that creativity flowing again is by taking action. Complete all those chores you have been putting off. Once you have completed enough actions, big or small, your energy and thirst for life will also return.

So, for your fitness maybe it's not enough to just join a gym. Instead, you hire a personal trainer who comes to your house three or five days a week to workout with you. Maybe you sign up for a dance or martial arts class that you've always thought about doing. Do it! It could be something there that leads you to another fabulous adventure or opportunity. At the very least you'll get in shape and feel great about yourself and who knows where that will lead you!

If you've gotten comfortable in leggings and sweats, it's an easy trap to fall into, what would happen if you took every pair, threw them into a bag and either tossed them into a dumpster or donated them to a shelter? Don't give it a second thought; just do it. This is about challenging your normal way of thinking. The sweatpants are merely a symptom of something larger going on, like the extra weight you've put on or a lack of self-esteem in looking your best.

With your career, if you've been slacking off, do the thing that feels scariest and schedule a meeting with your boss to find out exactly where you're letting him or her down. Then, dedicate time to developing an action plan that will turn things around.

In your relationship, look where you take it for granted and step it up! Don't wait until it's gone to see that you need to make some changes.

Get back in charge of life and yourself by improving from a place of contentment. The most successful among us find happiness and fulfillment in the achievement of goals, not in "loaf time." Get real, get honest and get out of that normal frame of mind.

Empire-Building Exercise 2:

This is an easy one. Ready? Beat the sun up. I learned this one from my husband and it works.

Yes, that's it! Wake up before the sun rises. Every morning. Regardless of whether you sleep alone, next to your partner, or have a toddler or pet who's prone to joining your bed. You'll start to feel a sense of pride in the fact that you're disciplined and not a lazy sleepyhead. You'll find that extra time you need to get those unfinished chores completed. And you'll feel like you at least did something, merely with the act of waking up early.

This means you have to get off social media and get to bed earlier. I am not telling you to get less sleep. I am quite the opposite from those other "hustling" guys and girls out there who promote never sleeping. Get rest. Bottom line, you are more functional and clear-headed when you have proper rest. You can actually get more done. Get a good night's sleep in order to get up, get out and meet the world head on!

Empire-Building Exercise 3:

Write a list of your strengths and weaknesses. Write three examples of what an enemy would do or say to attack your strong suit. Write three examples of what an enemy would do or say to play into your weakness or make you more vulnerable and susceptible to them.

Do the same now for a true friend. Write three ways you envision they would help you build upon your strengths. Now write three ways they would steer you away from your weakness and another three ways they could help turn your weaknesses into strengths.

Chapter 9

Your Royal Court

The people you surround yourself with aren't just your friends and coworkers, they're assets. This might sound strange if you're used to thinking of assets as physical, tangible things, like money, houses and cars. But I consider the greatest assets in my empire to be people.

These assets, positive, contributing team members, all fill roles within your empire. Much like a traditional king and queen had a royal court with appointed members to execute certain tasks. The court jester would entertain the masses. The page would serve as the communicator. The maid of honor would attend to the queen's needs, and the knights or royal guards would protect and defend you at all costs. You want these!

Besides using these analogies here, you better not tell your best friend that she's your lady in waiting or sit atop a throne and demand that your sarcastic brother perform a dance for you as the jester. Something tells me it wouldn't go over well.

Rather, picking your royal court is about an inherent knowledge of who fits into your life and your empire, and why they're there in the first place. This can be a challenging task since it forces you to examine not just the quantity of your relationships, but the quality.

Less Is More

Grant and I have a mission of reaching all the people this planet. And we consider anyone who wants to improve their life to the fullest potential as being within our empire as well.

Our inner circle, though, is watertight. Purposely designed that way to keep enemies out and the allies in. But if you're a friend to me, you might as well be my family. I will do anything for you. I'm not perfect, and chances are I will forget your birthday but when you need me, I show up. They can ALWAYS count on me. I would drop everything and move mountains for a friend in need. I am loyal and honorable and so are my friends.

But our friends don't just know they're special and appreciated, they carry their weight. If one falls down, we'll be there for the other — but only for so long. It may sound cold and harsh but I surround myself with competent and contributing people. I cannot afford to come off of my goal of trying to "save the world" to go rescue dramatic people who call on me every time they get a paper cut! Go rub some ointment on it and get on with it!

At the end of the day, your empire is only as strong as the people you let into it. Your royal court needs to continuously prove themselves to be assets or else it's time to go. Again, I know it's a tough pill to swallow. Who doesn't have that lifelong friend who isn't really on the same page as you and you have nothing in common anymore but you feel obligated to keep them around? Maybe it's an employee who shows a lot of loyalty but can't produce, continues to make mistakes and is bringing down your organization as a result.

Perhaps the hardest relationships to examine are those with your own family. They say that blood is thicker than water, however if you're trying to build and grow an empire, you need to be careful how much slack you allow for certain family members who are otherwise a drag on your resources and energy. Again, this is a personal conversation that you need to have first with yourself and your spouse. Unfortunately, you are probably nodding your head and can think of at least one person who fits that description to a tee.

As queen, I take the responsibility of picking our inner circle with the utmost care. I run all of the inner circle activities, whether that means corporate outings with Grant's companies, holiday and social time, family outings and trips, social affairs, schooling, personal trainers, security, housekeeper, babysitters and anyone who works inside the household, just to name a few. All are extensively vetted by me before anyone comes near Grant or my children.

I depend on the royal court to do their jobs diligently and professionally. If the people I've chosen can't handle being on the team, then they're off the roster. I need complete competence around us. Quite often, our environment can go from fun to all-out intense pressure-cooker moments depending on what's going on at the time. It might sound ruthless, but when you're trying to take down huge targets, you don't have the patience to waste on people that will get you slaughtered. There is a reason only the select few make it to the Navy Seals or Army Special Forces. These elites only want the best on their team. Not everyone has what it takes to fit into your culture, your rules and your empire.

You'll want to dedicate time reviewing the relationships in your life and coming to terms with them. Do this exercise objectively and remove emotion from the equation. When you know certain people fall short or you spot red flags in your friend's character flaws, it is vital you STOP making justifications in your mind about it. You need to surround yourself with "Special Forces" in order for you to rise to your own occasion. A team holds each other accountable and truly strives for greatness. Greatness isn't made drunk in a club, period.

Having A Heart: A Lesson

Grant and I made a pact a long time ago that, *"No matter what, it's you and me in the end."* It means that we now accept that people will come and go in our lives, but the one thing that won't change is us.

There have been times when someone we thought was an asset turned out to be a liability. This is someone who brings personal problems inside of our empire, who creates drama, and who seeks to detract us from our greater mission — knowingly or unknowingly. It creates tension between Grant and me.

There have been several times I've granted second, third, even fourth chances to people who aren't pulling their weight. And all the while the very act of doing so put a strain on my relationship. What's been the hardest to learn is that these nice, well-intentioned people are often the ones who've hurt me the most. Better to get rid of them early on before they wreak more havoc later. It's my responsibility to architect the empire. You better believe I make sure the king is surrounded by the very best of everything and that includes people, especially people.

Choosing Roles

Everyone's royal court will look a little different, which is important to keep in mind as you build your empire and team of assets within it.

KING - Grant Cardone. The man, the icon, the magnate, the real estate tycoon, leader, soldier, warrior, and hero to all.

QUEEN - That's me, Elena Cardone. Empire-builder, architect, magic maker, overseer of the royal court, caretaker for allies, rearing the children, and procuring assets among many other things.

ROYAL ADVISOR - Sheri Hamilton, Chief Operating Officer of Cardone Enterprises and one of the most loyal, badass chicks you'll ever meet. She helps operate the business, and Grant to run seamlessly, no matter what challenges we face. Sheri runs a tight ship when Grant is off sailing new seas. She is one of a few people I can truly trust. A rare commodity in this ever-growing world of "success" all too often built upon illusions and lies.

NOBEL KNIGHT - Ryan Tseko, not only is he one of the pilots of the Gulfstream G550 but also the Portfolio Manager for Cardone Capital that has close to $1 billion in assets under management.

ROYAL KNIGHT - Jarrod Glandt, Vice President of Sales and Business Development for Cardone Enterprises, co-host of Young Hustlers, and the guy who has the guts, and enthusiasm to match Grant in bringing our vision of helping eight billion people a reality.

PRINCESSES - Sabrina and Scarlett Cardone, our little ladies who are so bold and smart, who impress me every day with their strength, intellect and ability to "hold down the fort" as Grant and I grow our empire. They also host their own show, The 10X Kids, giving advice to other kids.

THE MESSENGERS - All our incredible staff who believe in us and help get our message out to the masses.

ROYAL SUBJECTS - The employees, investors, and fans of Cardone Enterprises, 10X Media Productions, Cardone Training and Cardone Capital. We honestly wouldn't be anywhere without their support, energy, and belief in our ability to grow, reinvest and make magic happen.

THE 10X RULE - *"The 10X Rule"* was a book written by my husband, which states that in order to achieve targets, you must multiply your efforts by ten if you are to actually have a chance of hitting your goals. These are the laws of the land that govern our empire.

A Virtual Empire

If you're just starting out, or have found yourself in a position where you don't physically have anyone you'd want as part of your empire, that's okay. Instead, you'll want to create what I call a virtual empire, assigning roles to people you might not have yet met whose principles and values you admire, and which you can bring into your life, and empire.

So, let's say you'd want Grant or me to serve as your royal advisor for all things career or empire building related. While a phone call or text might not be possible, it is feasible to watch our videos, listen to our podcasts, read our books or follow us on social media. Grant and I particularly pride ourselves on bringing our very best to all of the content we produce, with the hopes of setting an example for other couples and empire builders. We can always be found on all socials as @elenacardone and @grantcardone.

Starve the Enemies

As we wrap up this chapter, I'll leave you with this: I don't agree that you should keep your friends close, but your enemies closer. Your royal court are your allies, assets, and the people who are going to have your back provided you do the same for them. Giving the enemies of your empire your attention and energy is exactly what they want and exactly what they won't get from this empire. I prefer to starve them out. Pour your resources into the things, people and places that give back to you.

Empire-Building Exercise: Your Coronation Dinner

Imagine that you're in charge of creating the most fabulous dinner party on the face of the planet. Let's just make it your coronation as king or queen of your newly inherited crown and you get to invite whomever you want. Who would you invite? And where would they sit? How many are at your dinner table? Who would be worthy? This is no ordinary dinner party; this is the kind where deals happen, memories are made, and a good time is had by all. You'd choose wisely, wouldn't you? You have to prioritize. Where would you place your joker friends when you now need to care for the knights and royal elites who help you grow, expand, protect and defend?

This is the frame of mind you'll want to adapt as you consider the roles within your royal court. Use this exercise to plan out a seating chart for your coronation. How many get to sit at the king and queen's table? Why are they there and what is their placement in relation to you? Who sits at the surrounding tables and why? It's up to you and what kind of empire you want to build. Remember this not a real event so don't worry about actually hurting anyone's feelings. See if you have any realizations while doing this.

Are you giving seats away just because some longtime friend is entitled?

I often speak of sacrifices. The unfortunate reality is that as you really start to focus and grow, your friends might not see you as much, and some might fall by the wayside. The true friends will be there for you through it all and push you to be great even if it means sacrificed time.

These are my closest and most cherished friends because they understand their value to me and don't demand time as some sort of proof. You must start to consider who is in your life, why they are there, and who and what you are for them as well.

My friends are all queens of their empires and we mutually treat each other with love and respect. A queen hangs with a fellow queen for a reason.

I can ask the guys the same question though. Who do you surround yourself with? A bunch of jokers or other kings who truly inspire and push you to supremacy.

When you're done, share your results with your partner to see who he or she would invite. Are your lists the same, or different?

Chapter 10
Lighten Up!

All work and no fun makes for a very dull empire. In fact, if you don't incorporate a sense of play into your empire-building, you're probably going to throw in the towel, run for the hills, tap out, surrender, and wind up with no empire at all. Humor, laughter, a sense of ease; these are key ingredients that can help keep your empire going strong when things get tense. It's important to find a way to inject a little bit of lightness into each day whether it's an inside joke with your partner, or planning a fun outing with the whole family. It doesn't have to break the bank, either.

Grant and I spent a lot of time doing grunt work while we rebuilt our empire following the recession of 2008. As I mentioned previously, there were no vacations. All we had was humor and the fun we created just being with each other. That's why it surprised me when a couple of years ago, Grant confessed that he was ready for his first vacation in thirteen years!

He deserved it and I wanted to help him celebrate our victories. But if you know anything about me by now, you can be sure I included some empire building into the mix. A tactic that you, too, can incorporate into your next set of plans.

Get It Done (In The Sun)

Picking where to go was the easy part. St. Barts is my absolute favorite place for a good time. I was determined to give Grant the best vacation he'd ever experienced. Which is why you might find it strange that I surprised him with a beautiful, ten-bedroom, beachfront, compound estate so that several of his clients and associates could join us. Yes, it was a working vacation with plenty of swimming, paddle boarding, boogie boarding, rented yachts, jet skis, incredible dinners, champagne and dancing on tabletops. It might not be right for everyone, or for every trip, but it allowed us to blend fun and business with some of our favorite people. Plus, if your husband is Grant Cardone, you know it's hard for him to turn off "hustle" mode.

Anyone married to a true entrepreneur knows that too much time off will only make them anxious and bored. And when an entrepreneurial beast gets bored, you better be strong enough to withstand those category-five hurricane force winds that will be aimed directly at you. So, people may accuse me of working Grant too much but I say my own survival is at stake here, people! Ultimately, I understand that production truly makes him happy. Why not make it all work to your advantage?

Coincidentally, it was in the heat of this vacation where the world felt like it was absolutely our oyster. We realized how easily we were able to acquiesce work with play — that maybe, after all, we could simultaneously travel for pleasure and get work done. Grant was astounded by how much work he was able to get done but even more astonished by how much fun he had. We fell deeper in love during that vacation. This trip alone made him determined to start traveling at least once a year if not more. For someone like me, who has had world travel on my goals list for so many years, I couldn't have been happier when I heard the news.

I was able to convince Grant we need to go global with our travels. Enter our new global-equipped Gulfstream G550. All from two weeks in St. Barts and taking a gamble on a play that couldn't have had a better outcome if I planned it myself. Wink. Wink.

Find A Way

If you're still in the early stages of building your empire, then I get it. I don't expect you to just be able to zip off to the Caribbean with your honey and kids in tow or to drop everything for the sake of a little bit of time off. There's a time for work, and a time for play.

But, this is my challenge to you, can you find a way to make, and be a good time? Even if you're capital resources are limited, try to envision ways you can bring a sense of lightness into your empire. I'm talking to you, Too Serious Sally and you also Too Serious Sam.

Be a Good Time

Being a good time for your partner isn't just about planning vacations or weekend trips with your family. Be pleasant! Be happy. When I show up to the office, you can bet your last dollar that I've got a smile spread across my face. It doesn't matter what kind of day I'm having at home or what challenges I might be facing. As empress and queen of my empire, I know that part of my role entails taking ownership of my outward appearances. It might sound silly to suggest that a good mood is part of that equation, but I firmly believe that if you allow your mind to focus on the positive, you'll show up in the world in a positive place.

Too frou-frou for you? Then, how about this: be kind to everyone you meet. You have no idea who might have the tip-off for your next multi-million dollar venture. Being kind is part of providing a good time for everyone around you. It's less about owing someone one of your dazzling smiles and more about knowing that when you spread joy, you make the world a better place. (If there ever were a case for "fake it till you make it," it'd be here.)

Most of my military friends hate when I say *"fake it till you make it"* but I'm not talking about the poser faking success to impress. The kind of "fake it" I'm talking about is getting up and forcing yourself to smile even when times are hard. Maybe a better way to phrase it would be "assume the position!"

Change how you treat yourself and others. Control your emotions a bit. The world doesn't revolve around you and your precious little feelings. No one cares how you feel about every delicate moment in your precious life. So stop being so selfish. Put your attention outward on others for a change, and see if you have any power whatsoever to positively impact someone else's life! Can you actually make someone else smile? You can always go back to being a grouch but let it be your choice to be that way and not the grouch controlling you.

One might call it hocus pocus but everything starts with the little things in life. When you start choosing your behavior rather than reacting on some impulse you can't control, you are mastering life and its outcome. When you take that one step further and can influence the behaviors of others in a favorable way, now, you have mastered what it takes to build, control and expand an empire. Never underestimate the effect you create. Power is power.

Empire-Building Exercise:
Go Play!

Create a list of at least five ways you can incorporate fun into your relationship. If you're well into your empire and have the funds, consider planning a trip. Where would you go? Who would you bring and what would you do with your time? Remember to include activities for the kids and business associates. Play. Be a good time... in every sense of the word! Be that partner that your partner wants to brag about because you are so freaking fun and cool.

The more willing you are to be a good time with your partner, the more he or she will want to spend time with you. Find ways to intermingle business with pleasure so no one has to feel the pressure of choosing between the two. True partnerships make life easier. Don't let life get too serious, remember to have fun and carry on.

PART
FOUR

Defend Your Empire

"To be prepared for war is one of the most effective means of preserving the peace."
—George Washington

Chapter 11
Enemies Of The Empire

If there was a chapter in this book I really didn't want to write, this one would be it.

Enemies. Who wants to have them? Definitely not me. Enemies are not the same as haters. Enemies are way worse and a threat that you need to prepare for.

I'll be the first to admit it, I like being liked. I've always been a people person, and have always appreciated that special, and often rare connection, that can happen when someone truly "gets" you. It makes me feel appreciated, inspires me to push, and deliver more in life and as a queen. I am aware that I am not supposed to crave being liked and I'm not supposed to care what anyone thinks of me, but I would be lying if I said that I didn't. I do consider this a weakness in myself and I have learned to work with it. I've built up a body armor and learned how to take a metaphorical hit by enemies (and haters alike) but I would be lying if I said it didn't hurt.

I also dislike confrontation. I hate to even admit that. I prefer to keep things within my control as harmonious as possible. Grant, on the other hand, loves his haters, and takes their wrath as a sign he's become less obscure and better known. While it might be hardwired into us as humans to want to fit in, the fact of the matter is, there are enemies everywhere.

Your success instills in them a sense of inferiority, and so, they will do whatever it takes to bring you down. If you don't train your eye to notice them, they can attack and destroy your empire faster than you can see them coming. All the more reason why it's essential to build yours carefully and strategically from the ground up.

First Things First: Enemies are Inevitable

Let me start by saying that Grant and I know how lucky we are to have each other. We've got shared goals, mutual respect, and a lot of love between us and our kids. Appreciating what we have, and knowing how rare that is, is one of the reasons why I think we've been able to stick it out through both good and bad times. We're constantly working on ourselves, our marriage and our empire. We don't let the little stuff get to us and we make an effort to buffer against the bigger blows life doles out.

That said, I'm not living under a rock and I see the hateful negativity that can float through on social media. I'm attacked for my religion, being a woman who supports and backs my husband, my love of guns, for being a Second Amendment advocate, as well as wanting to open a Congressional Federal Investigation into the correlation between psychiatric drugs and random acts of senseless violence, to being criticized for how I look, my annoying personality, for my wealth and also hated because I love and support the police and military just to name a few.

Do I like what these people have to say? No! But hurt or scared feelings are only emotions and you're ultimately responsible for how you feel about any given situation. The easiest thing to do is delete, block and alert police if needed. I actually have to focus on my empire and off the threat. I definitely don't engage in a back and forth online bash sessions as I'm not looking to antagonize anyone. As you know by now, I'm trying to build an empire and help as many people as I can along the way, so I can't afford to get distracted.

Think of these people as barking dogs chasing the tires of your car as you roll down the street. They're too dumb to know you could roll over them. But if you keep going, they eventually tire out and give up.

Develop Your Approach

What stings the most is knowing that the most dangerous enemy is the one you personally let in and not some barking dog who's throwing hate from the sidelines.

These enemies have already found a way into your empire. Like a bomb set off in a building versus just outside the door, they cause a lot of internal damage, devastation, and can leave you feeling vulnerable. When you do find an enemy like this, you need to reassess your weaknesses. This requires getting real and humble with yourself about the bad decisions you made that allowed it to happen in the first place. It's also one of the best ways to identify your empires as a whole. Is it really as strong as you think it is? The impact of an enemy never feels good, but rebuilding and learning from your mistakes do.

In truth, I have only a few true enemies. These are people who've severely betrayed the trust I placed in them and who've sought to destroy my family or my empire. Enemies are evil. While some people argue that it's better to forgive than hold a grudge, I can tell you that real enemies are as good as dead to me. I will hold my head high if I'm ever in the same space as them, but I'll never acknowledge their presence. Once you are on the enemy list, you never come off.

It's not healthy to walk around holding in anger, which is easy to do if you let your enemies get under your skin without a way to detach.

Violence is also not an option unless of course there is a direct physical threat, but I hope nothing like that ever occurs.

Still, you've got to determine how you'll handle your enemies before they handle you. You might even use a few different approaches depending on the situation at hand, especially if you uncover a traitor down the line. I don't play chess but I'm told the Queen is the most powerful piece due to her ruthlessness and her ability to move in any direction on the board. The queen is powerful, should never be underestimated, and should be utilized accordingly in building an empire. Remember, I am talking about queens, not girls or princesses.

Elena Cardone: Architect

A lot of the work I do happens behind the scenes. In fact, many of the deals that you'll see Grant orchestrate were the result of having cultivated the ideas, relationships, having vetted allies, and devising the plans and projects that make their way into our empire. Once I convince Grant to buy in on an idea, I send him out as my trusted soldier into the field to execute the mission.

When he comes home, the house is clean, he is happily greeted by the family, he is fed and treated like the hero of our home. This is done no matter what. I could be mad at him, annoyed or whatever, but I'm putting that aside when it comes to keeping us intact until we have a chance to work it out. Remember with every action you are either creating or destroying. You don't have to destroy when you are angry. It is possible to still create while getting through it.

It's easy to see the upside of our hard work. We share a lot of our life with our fans on social media and we're proud of the lifestyle that success has brought our way. That is, after all, the nature of social media. Post what looks good and sweep the ugly stuff under the rug like the transparency of being burned in life or in a deal and being sued as a result. Unfortunately, this has happened a few too many times, though believe me, we're wiser for it.

The Grand Slam Gone Wrong

I'll carefully share with you a story of what happens when you don't properly vet your inner circle and get burned in the process. This book is all about showing you the lessons we've learned with the hopes that you won't repeat our mistakes as you grow your own empires.

In this particular "mission" as I call it, I had arranged a partnership with a firm that wanted to do business with Grant. It required a tremendous investment of assets and resources from our end. However, it would have been our biggest deal to date. I loved all of the players involved and could only see the upside. All parties involved were going to win. Sure, there were a few red flags I had detected from the other side but I ignored those. The dangling carrot looked too good to pass on and I was a hungry little rabbit! Hint: if it's too good to be true, it probably is.

Not only that, I was proud and excited to have been the mastermind behind the scenes. I'd pulled off some victories and major wins in the past but this was going to be my real grand slam.

The deal was signed and we were a go. All of our teams went eagerly to work on this new project. A couple of months had passed, and instead of returning to the table each day with vigor and enthusiasm, my team was exhausted. The people at the other end of the rope had started to reveal their hideous nature. In fact, my team wanted out. I said, *"Oh, no, there will be none of that."* If there's one thing Grant and I are known for, it's that we don't quit. Not on our marriage, not on our deals, not on our kids or on anything else in life. I wanted that doggone carrot and I went blind. I laid out plans B, C, and D, then smoothed things over as best as I could while we course corrected our ships.

Another month went by and my team attempted to tap out, begging to put this thing to rest. *"Sorry",* I told them, *"but no."* I knew it was tough but I knew they could pull through. I used my best motivational speech and sent them back to the battlefield.

Meanwhile, I went back to the people who ran this organization that had so desperately wanted to work with Grant to see what happened. My investigative observations led me to the conclusion that several people below the heads of the company were threatened by Grant. They were afraid they would lose their jobs once their true value surfaced. So, they poisoned the well so to speak. These people spread outrageous lies about us in order to cover their losses. They flat-out tried to destroy us.

By the end, we were so entangled with the firm that when the bomb finally went off our empire was rattled from the inside out. It was my own fault, I had lost focus and got derailed from our own company's purpose. The blowup disrupted our organization and we took a hit.

They won their petty battle but it was ugly. The team was bloodied and bruised. Despite my enthusiasm and genuine desire to do a good thing, I'd failed. While it would have been just as easy to pinpoint the blame on any number of people involved, I took the heat. It was my idea to entertain this partnership in the first place. It was I who was mesmerized by the trojan horse, freely opened the gates, let it in, and watched as it unleashed havoc.

Did it hurt? Absolutely. Not just emotionally, but financially. And no matter how far up the totem pole you are, nothing rattles your soul quite like knowing you made a misjudgment of character. It can make you question the other important decisions you make each day. If you're not careful, it sends you down a rabbit hole of self-doubt, especially when you thought that business partner was a friend. It burned and it hurt on a very deep level. It was an extremely painful moment for me when that mission failed so catastrophically.

Being the queen, it's my duty to protect my empire. Friendship isn't a joke to me, and it's not something I take for granted. I defend the ones I care about, and I know that my true friends would do the same for me. But once you discover a weak link or traitor in your empire, no matter how big their smile is, you've got to get rid of them. You want that person as far away from your empire as possible.

Still, when this deal blew up, the betrayal felt so deep it gutted me. I'll never show it publicly, I'm much stronger internally than I perhaps look externally. Mistakes are how we learn. But I hate giving the enemy the satisfaction of seeing the pain of my loss even if briefly.

If it wasn't for the strength of my relationship with Grant during this time, I honestly don't know where I'd be today. While the details of this deal might seem vague to you, I assure you that it was a dark moment in my life. I HATE failing. I hate losing. I hate even more someone trying to threaten my king and I had been checkmated.

Paradoxically, it made me want a normal life. Something easy where everything wasn't a constant challenge. I admit I wanted to give up, just sit back, relax, and even worse, withdraw from everyone and trust no one ever again. I knew it wasn't the answer. Grant knew it, too.

Grant, and my family were my rocks during this time. Yes, setbacks hurt. I've got enough scars to show for them, but you've got to use that hurt to fuel your forward momentum. I picked myself up with a smile on my face and determined as all hell. They may have won the battle but I will always win the war! The war that we fight every day to help even more people and be even more successful. Right or wrong, it fuels me to be better than those people and watching our success without them will be even sweeter.

In The Face of Enemies, Rise Again

Recovering from a setback can't be about feeling sorry for yourself. We get stronger by facing adversity and new challenges, not shying away from them. Which is exactly why once I was done being hurt, I began to brainstorm more ways Grant and I could expand our empire.

At first, I thought we have to get global exposure and get all of Grant's material known internationally. This was the birth of getting a plane equipped to take us anywhere in the world. Then the idea suddenly came that we could set up Grant Cardone affiliates globally. Hence the Cardone Licensing Program. And our global tour will launch at the end of 2018.

As if I wasn't excited enough by this concept, my next idea literally blew me away. I would turn those feelings of wanting to never trust anyone again and withdrawing from life into the complete opposite. I decided I wanted to be the big guy who doesn't hurt the little guy. I was sick of having just witnessed what a big firm gets away with and how they treat people.

That's when it hit me, Grant and I have the opportunity through real estate to help all the "underdogs" or "little people" just like us, who only want a chance to get in the game. I am not a conspiracy theorist, but I'm telling you the system is rigged against us. The people like you and I are purposefully excluded by the big boys at the top. The system wants to keep you misinformed about many things, but especially about money. Without going off more on my conspiracy theories, I'll just say this, Grant and I both individually started at the bottom and found our way up. We have been transparent about our process and our journey. We will continue to be, so others can join us if they choose. The underdogs united can be bigger, stronger and better together. Disrupting the system and taking as many underdogs with us straight to the top, became, and remains my new full-time mission.

Enter Cardone Capital. A real estate fund open to you, for both accredited and non-accredited investors. The structure of which allows everyone to get a piece of the pie and scale toward a massive level.

Cardone Capital has a portfolio of five-thousand apartment units at the publishing of this book. I couldn't be prouder of Grant and the team for making it what it is today, and what it'll be tomorrow. The goal is to get ten-thousand units which will equate to a billion in assets. The next goal is forty-thousand units and make it a multi-billion-dollar empire. And leaving all who partook in the empire, extremely rich! We can get there on our own but it will take a decade if not longer ¬— or we can get there with you and together we can rise.

The more capital we raise, the faster we can acquire assets. The faster we acquire assets, the quicker everyone will hit pay dirt. It's like in the game of Monopoly. Whoever owns Park Place and Boardwalk always wins the game. Therefore, the people who invest with us are not only our partners, allies, teammates, and friends, they are part of a movement. We are rooting for them as much as they are rooting for us. We are proud to walk amongst you and we will fight for you.

I love our 10Xers and Cardone Capital Investors. I would not have an empire without you. I'll protect you as I would my own family. At the end of the day, your greatest asset, aside from time, is your ability to love and help one another. Love, I believe, conquers all. You guys give me a purpose and motivation to rise up and push for something greater. From the bottom of my heart, I thank you for your support and, of course, I love and appreciate you all. Now, let's get to the top!

Success is what will deliver you from victimhood. Cardone Capital never would have come to fruition had I not had such a massive failure blow up in my face. You've got to latch onto your purpose in order to keep pushing forward and not let the hard knocks make you jaded and introverted.

In the course of life and business, you'll bruise. You'll bleed. Not only will you knock your own self down stumbling over your own two feet, but you'll get punched down plenty more times by the enemy. They are relentless in their efforts for destruction and won't hesitate to deliver a roundhouse kick to your head, catch you with an additional liver shot on your way down and put you in a choke hold just for safe measure! There will not be a referee to pull someone off of you. Whether you shrink, quit, or allow your empire to be destroyed, that is ultimately a choice left to you. Your enemy can't destroy your empire unless you let them. They get stronger by making your weaker. So get back up, smile, breathe, put your hands back up and fight your war. Then have your comeback and claim your rightful title, champ! No matter what battles they may win, NEVER let them conquer you!

Don't Hate; Contemplate

Lastly, a word about hate. It's an ugly word, and even though we used the word haters in this chapter in a rather cavalier way, I'm talking about the actual force and energy of hate itself.

Don't hate your enemies. Never wish them harm. OK, a quick short fantasy here and there won't kill you, but overall, don't waste the energy. Your best revenge, if you want to call it that, is to stay totally focused on you, your empire, your partner, your business, your happiness, your success, and your life. Find more ways to give, and when you think you can't give anymore, give again. Get so busy producing with your life, you have no spare time to spend on them. It makes them go berserk when they can't upset you. They are trying to create an effect on you and when you eliminate their game, they eventually lose interest and go antagonize someone else.

Yes, you can certainly use the criticism your enemies spew at you as fuel for the fire but your motivation must be bigger than proving people wrong. As discussed many times in the book, you are either creating or destroying an empire. Enemies, in the form of financial calamity, detractors, trojan horses, and bad decisions will be waiting at every corner. Instead of preparing each time to fight, repurpose your thoughts, avoid losses, and stay the course.

Empire-Building Exercise: Sweep Your Empire for Enemies

Remember while there are a lot of bad apples out in the world, most people are good and worth loving.

STEP 1 - Review your associates and connections. Jot down any red flags you're aware of but have otherwise tried to ignore. For example, drinks too much, does drugs, cheats on the spouse, is late all the time, hits their kids, steals from the boss, lies, has lots of accidents, lives in a cluttered, chaotic environment, dangerous things occur around them, gossips about mutual friends, etc. These are just some I thought of to get you started. And, sure, we all find ourselves in a few of these less serious categories from time to time, but look at the big, glaring, obvious people that spring to mind over and over as you read your list.

STEP 2 - Take a step backward. How did these people get to where they are in your empire? Write down when you spotted red flags. What were they? What did you say to yourself to excuse that behavior? On a sidenote, if one of your excuses was *"it's not my business"* then you still haven't adopted the empire mindset. It is the business of the king and queen to know everything that takes place within the castle walls. It is up to the emperors to decide what riff-raff stays and what goes. But if you allow it to stay, don't act shocked when the landmine blows up. Unlike the Hollywood version, real-life landmines don't give warning when you step on one. There is no click alerting you to stand completely still while you get to say your last goodbyes. There is no special bomb-diffusing team showing up to give you a false hope that you may actually be rescued. No, the riff-raff you allow into your empire, much like the landmine, will do what it was designed to do which is to cause as much destruction as possible without warning.

Observe the types of things you use as excuses for these people so you can recognize when you do it again in the future. This will become your own red flag that will alert you there is a potential problem lurking. Preventing accidents is just as crucial as scoring home runs.

STEP 3 - Now, review your observations, and decide what is the best way to handle this person/people. If it's a matter of having a conversation, schedule it. If it's time to let this person go, waste no time in making your intentions known and remove them from your empire.

STEP 4 - Regroup with the other members of your inner circle and have them sweep their circles to see if there are other weak spots within the empire that need reassessment. Again, this isn't a witch-hunt but you'll know who doesn't belong.

Chapter 12

How To Destroy An Empire

As I've said, destruction of an empire is often an inside job. I've seen even the best of marriages crumble under the weight of vices left unchecked, and families ripped apart by bad habits that have no place inside a home.

Mostly, these are mental takedowns. Internal crusaders in search of a weak commitment to the cause and knowing that with a little bit of push and pull, you'll be subject to their siren song. In other cases, they're outside influences, the kind you can take anywhere and that love to travel. It goes without saying that drugs, alcohol and other addictions are serious issues.

For the rest of us self-sabotage is an unfortunately common occurrence. There are ways around it if you learn to observe the cues. The mind is an incredibly powerful and insightful tool, capable of just about anything if you'll allow it to. Take back your power, and your time, attention, and health by avoiding these empire-destroying vices and habits.

Alcohol and Drugs

Excessive alcohol and drugs are no friends of the empire, not within the throne, and definitely not within the royal court. It may be unpopular to mention this, but it is true. The more responsibility you take, the clearer you will need your mind to be. You need to be sharp, alert and smart to make quality, precision decisions. If you're like me, you've done enough drugs and alcohol in your life that it's time to play a newer, bigger game in life. The more you can accomplish with a sober mind, the stronger you will be. It takes real guts to confront life head-on.

It doesn't matter if you have a high tolerance for getting high and drunk, and I don't care what you say you can and can't handle when it comes to this stuff, if you know these are problem areas for you, and for most people they are, avoid them at all costs.

Gossip

Gossip is cheap, easy, and tasteless. A habit not fit for the crown. As you continue to expand your empire, you'll want to be mindful of how you carry yourself. If that person was standing next to you, would you be talking about them unfavorably? Make it your goal to only speak positively about the people in your life. If you can't, then that's a red flag indicating their behavior might not be worthy of holding court.

When you rise to the top, people will look to you as a role model or an example of how to be. You must be strong enough to be trustworthy. No one likes or trusts a gossip. You will lose your allies and create unnecessary dramas in your life which otherwise could be easily avoided. You must be disciplined enough to keep your mouth shut. You must also have the courage to stand up for everyone in your empire if someone dares even attempt to criticize them to you. That is another form of people trying to destroy your empire. They will try to attack and dismember your friends, staff, partners, business affairs, etc. Be willing to strike a hard blow and make an example of these folks so no one dares threaten your crew ever again!

You will earn respect and loyalty as an extra bonus.

Negativity

Negativity breeds more negativity. This goes for your thoughts like how and what you speak about, and with. These patterns of behavior keep you distracted from reaching your goals. Get rid of it!

A Lack of Purpose

If you put your purpose to the wayside, it creates a void that tends to stay dark. Having a purpose isn't some rah-rah way to get you pepped up. It literally means taking stake in your own life and deciding what you stand for and letting that empower you to greatness.

Attention To Your Goals (and Money)

The things we pay attention to, grow. If you've got your mind set on other people's opinions, reality TV or complaining, that means it's not set on your goals or your money. Get your goals and your money right by getting your focus right. Taking a break to assess who's doing what in a tabloid or on Facebook when you should be building your empire isn't just a waste of time, it's an insult to your empire as a whole. Spend your time learning everything you need in order to skill up at your job. If you are in business, find a mentor like Grant and go deep studying everything about what he or she has to say on the subject. If the mentor is good, you should be able to apply what you learn immediately to life and see a change fairly quick.

Empire-Building Exercise: Kill Your Masters

There's a lot to be said about burning bridges so that you can't go back. It's easier to walk away from a bad relationship or employer than it is the habits and outworn beliefs we've cultivated over time.

Still, I wonder what would happen if you were to go cold turkey on your worst offenders? You know, the habits that you claim are so easy to give up. What if someone were to challenge you, as I am now? Would I have to pry the cigarettes, booze, sweets, drugs, TV, porno, social media or whatever other distractions you use out of your cold, dead, hands?

Give it a try. If you can't tackle all of the things I've suggested here, pick one way you can get healthier, either mentally, spiritually and physically today. Your empire and future successes depend on it.

Chapter

13

Hold Down The Fort

Magic. I know a thing or two about it. In fact, you could even say it is one of my specialties. What I'm talking about is the behind-the-scenes wizardry that goes into almost everything I do.

I'm not talking about casting spells, though a queen should always have a few tricks up her sleeve. Rather, I mean the illusion of calm, cool and collected in the midst of chaos or what I call holding down the fort.

Holding down the fort is exactly that. It means when one of you gets busy and has to work late, miss your child's birthday party or invite a business partner to your anniversary dinner, you cover for each other. You don't get mad or cause a huge upset and tell the kids how mama or papa has failed them again. Yes, those actions would certainly put you in the destroying an empire category.

You handle the kids so they understand their role in the family is to support the family at all costs. This means there are times sacrifices must be made in order to have the good life. It means they are actively contributing team members who know their mother or father are superheroes saving the world and also providing for the family. They know it's their job to do well in life and make it OK for the parents to be gone from time to time. Our kids know that Papa is a real man who loves, protects and provides for all of us and he is treated with respect. They know this because I have reared them this way and our home is filled with a calmness and love. They never feel abandoned.

It goes deeper than having well-behaved children though, it's about understanding each other's expectations as a family unit so that we all get our needs met, beyond money.

This is the life of being married to an entrepreneur. We are all a team and I'm proud of the way we operate as one. When he is away he knows he can count on me to run a smooth, tight ship where everyone is thriving and vice versa.

Rainbows, Unicorns, and Grant Cardone

It was Grant who said it first, *"I make magic happen."* As the wife of someone with an incredible amount of energy and power, it requires that I have even more. I have to be able to not only handle everything that he encompasses but also pivot, adapt and change gears at a moment's notice.

This entails a lot of different things. For starters, there are people who want to attack Grant, but are too cowardly so they'll come after me. The insults I can handle but threats I take seriously and I am prepared to protect myself and my children by any means.

But, it requires a sound mind, and a definite sense of self, as well as the awareness of what's happening. People who are ruthless and soulless will often do whatever it takes in an undermining way. That includes indirect attacks that you've got to recognize as they unfold. Plus, if you know anything about me, you can be damn sure I'll be just as ruthless to protect my husband and kids.

Then, there's the business of being Grant. That means if I get an 8pm text saying that executive so-and-so is coming over for dinner and have a meal and bottle of wine decanted within the next thirty minutes, I'm on it. It doesn't matter if I'm exhausted, without makeup, in pajamas and about to put the kids to bed. Elena, all-star wife and queen of the empire needs to make an appearance once more. All without a grudge, without complaints and knowing that it benefits our empire bottom line. Grant does not hang with people just to waste time. If he deems it important to have someone over, I do not question it for even a second.

This means to get food ordered and delivered once I kiss my girls goodnight. Then, dash into my closet to change out of the jammies, into the bathroom for a quick dab of lipstick and mascara, and back into our living room-bar area to pour those glasses of wine. When Grant and his guests enter a half hour later, there I am, elegant and smiling, as if it were flawless, almost magical.

Before you go and peg me as a simple little housewife who waits on her husband, know that there are plenty of other women out there who wouldn't lift a finger for their families. They feel they're owed something, or that serving their husbands in a domestic way is old-fashioned and sexist. Again, we're talking about empire building here. When you know your purpose you become tuned into the fact that it's not just about sharing a last name or a bedroom, it's about contributing to the greater good of the collective unit.

Even minute activities such as putting together dinner at the last minute become important, since it's the micro-actions we take that shape or shatter the bigger picture. When you're able to operate at this level even if it feels strange at first, you'll find there are fewer arguments because there's no time for them as you travel along a faster track to your own success.

Self-Care is Wealth Care

I'm a lifelong fan of shooting guns for sport. And recently I became attuned to various types of training with guns, knives, tactical courses, medical first aid, and also in self-defense. Fields that demand both precision and excellence in execution to the highest degree.

Training helps me in a few ways. It relaxes my mind, gives me an outlet to burn off steam and gives me a boost of confidence in dealing with life in general. It is the absolute best in assisting with the intense situations that come with running an almost half-a-billion-dollar empire. Times and tensions run high yet you must not show your hand. You must remain strong and forge forward. Training gives me the courage to fearlessly face anyone or anything and do it with class, dignity, and pride. I find the two worlds are very similar. I purposely train with the most elite in each field as I always insist on surrounding myself with only the very best. I make it a practice to never settle for less.

Self-care can take the form of spiritual training, a gym membership, a walk outside, eating well, getting enough rest, and surrounding yourself with ethical people. Doing things that serve you are not selfish.

Your empire, your partner, your kids, even your community all have needs. Meet yours first, in a healthy and productive way, and watch your contributions toward these other areas of your life grow and prosper.

Don't Get Stuck In First Gear

At the end of the day, I undergo a metamorphosis based on the needs of my empire. If I have to be the elegant, classy wife while out to dinner with clients, I'm doing it with a smile. If I need to be the fun, down-home chick motivating the troops at the office, I'm doing it with a smile. If I have to be Grant's confidant, lover, friend, assistant, ally, soldier, entertainer, wife extraordinaire or anything else you can think of — I'm doing it with a smile. If I need to pick up more than my share of the rope, go above and beyond for my kids, push myself to a higher level or stay laser-focused on a deal instead of taking a day off to have fun, I'm doing it with a smile.

No matter what the activity is, I'm bringing my "A" game. It's what is expected when you play at the top. It doesn't mean I'm perfect. There are times when generating much more than a grimace is really, really hard but I do it for my empire. I adore Grant. I know our place in this world is only as strong as our bond and what each of us brings to the table. He's a rare breed of human who wants to make life better for so many people. Loyalty, respect, honor and commitment are the least that I can offer to him in return for the many sacrifices he makes for our marriage and family.

It can be hard for some people to stay nimble for a number of reasons. They're comfortable doing things a certain way or they have a self-image they feel they have to maintain or they're not confident in their abilities to do things differently. But I'm here to tell you that being nimble and staying on your toes is an asset. The ability to become a chameleon with your own color palette is the way to navigate through life. Being seen bright and colorfully or blending in to be invisible when you want are both valuable tools. Know your own assets and don't be afraid to use them.

Empire-Building Exercise 1: Furnish Your Fort

It's much easier to hunker down and get things done if you're in a space that feels good.

What do <u>you</u> need to function at your most optimal? What uplifts, encourages and inspires <u>you</u>?

Home

- Find ways to make your personal space comfortable, relaxing and inviting. This can mean painting an accent wall, buying some bright throw pillows for your couch or getting fresh flowers. Make your bed. Start taking pride in the things you have, and clean up after yourself. Make your home, no matter the size, your castle.

- Clear out clutter, old paperwork, and clothes that either don't fit, physically, or don't fit the image of a queen or king. All of this stuff is a distraction to maintaining and building your empire. If it doesn't serve a purpose, get rid of it. Get used to letting go of things. It opens the doors to new things coming in. There is no scarcity of much of anything on this planet. Try going with less and free yourself up from old baggage, quite literally. You can always replace it later if you absolutely cannot live without.

- Remember that your home is your sanctuary, and should be treated as such. Keep in mind that energy permeates a space, so do your best to keep negativity out of yours. That can mean people, gossip, poor television and media choices, and even junk food.

Health

- Your health is truly the cornerstone of your empire. Be sure that you're up to date with things like an annual physical, teeth cleanings, and eye checkups. Make sure you're getting plenty of sleep, water, sunshine, fresh air plus healthy food and exercise. People that do this are less stressed and in general, happier and more even-tempered.

- If you've got bad habits, such as binging on junk food, smoking, drinking or drugs, do whatever it takes to nix those behaviors in the bud. Get rid of them. Pour all your newly freed-up time into empire building instead. You will hit your targets quicker.

- If you're already in a state of good physical health, do your best to not only maintain it but find ways to stretch and grow. It's important to be at the top of your game no matter what your age.

Wealth

- Having a baseline of how money works is critical in maintaining a healthy empire. If you're not sure where to start, pick up one of Grant's books or enroll in a program and get started on the path to learning. Remember, it doesn't matter how old you are, what counts is that you put forth the effort and commit to change.

- If you're financially savvy and have already established a baseline, look for ways to increase your income. Again, this is something Grant talks about a lot in his training programs, and particularly within his book, *"The 10X Rule."* If your income is at 10X levels and you're an accredited investor, consider an option like Cardone Capital, which can preserve and grow your wealth not only for today but for generations to come.

Community, Family, and Professional Resources

- Your royal court, also known as the friends, family, and employees who love you and want to see you succeed need a little tender loving care from time to time so be sure to foster the relationships that are healthy and mutually beneficial.

- Time is your most valuable asset, and unlike other areas, once it's spent, it's gone. If hiring a professional to clean or cook for you will take a load off of your back, do it. If you can't afford to bring in experts, examine your spending. Will a Netflix subscription give you more time to focus on your goals and your empire? Probably not. Would having a Saturday afternoon free to spend with your spouse while someone else takes care of the dirty dishes go a long way? You bet.

- Likewise, as queen or king of your empire, you'll be expected to do it all. Except you can't, at least not at once. You have to be smart enough to utilize people and delegate your jobs to others who can free you up to work on the things that are more valuable to you and buy your time back. It's another reason to pick wisely in your royal court. They will ensure the job you need completed is done as good, if not better, than you would have done it yourself.

Empire-Building Exercise 2:

Sit down with your family and come up with a family motto. Discuss what the family stands for and how you can each contribute. Make sure your let small kids contribute too so everyone is on the same page as a unit, no matter what the age. At the very least, making it OK when things change or a parent has to be away is a huge contribution in and of itself.

PART
FIVE

Expand Your Empire

"The only person you are destined to become
is the person you decide to be."
—Ralph Waldo Emerson

Chapter 14

Be A Gold Digger

A life of luxury, with a wealthy man to pay for it all?!

Despite the title, that's not what this chapter's about. Rather, I'm talking about taking that label and all of the negative connotation that comes with it and flipping it right back at any accuser who dares to put you in the corner. When you date and marry a rich man, it comes with the territory. I learned early on to embrace it and use it to my benefit.

On the other hand, there is value in mining for gold — in yourself, and in others.

"Those LA Girls..."

When Grant first moved to Los Angeles, which is where we met, a couple of his buddies and even some of his family members felt the need to warn him about falling prey to the notorious women of LA. Those beautiful, heartless, vindictive women only out for the money and nothing else.

One guy in particular, harbored a particular vendetta against me and tried to sabotage my extremely new relationship with Grant by yapping in his ear about me. He claimed I was a selfish, self-centered actress-type who would never care for anyone other than myself. He went on by saying that even if I were to be interested in Grant it would only be for his money.

Needless to say, this guy wasn't too happy when Grant and I started dating. But I had no idea this was happening behind my back.

Grant eventually told me what he was saying and I was completely floored. What he had failed to mention to Grant was he wanted to date to me! I was not interested in him and politely declined him numerous times. That same guy who was once so nice to me trying to get a date turned out to be a monster in disguise!

Then there were the family members who, being very protective indeed, had me under the same scrutiny for years. I won't lie, I was hurt. I'd been on my own since I was seventeen, earning my own money, paying my own mortgage and rent, figuring things out as I continued along in my journey. No one other than my parents had ever helped me financially through a hard time. And I always paid them back eventually. I'd had such a fierce independent streak. I didn't like someone making these types of claims and I certainly didn't like the drama. I was not about to prove myself to the friends and family of Grant Cardone, I can promise you that. Drama was always my first cue to bail in relationships and this was no different.

What Matters More?

At that point, I had to pause. The issue wasn't my relationship with Grant. It was my relationship with myself that was the problem.

To be specific, it was a vulnerability of mine that I'd allowed to be triggered by other people's actions and opinions. It is the complete opposite of self-confidence, and it will destroy even the most steely-looking person, man or woman, since it's an internal soft spot that must be managed and hardened.

Of course, who likes feeling weak or feeling like they have to suck up to someone? Definitely not me!

I tried to break up with Grant for the first time around this time as it seemed like this and a few other things were more work than I had bargained for. Of course, he didn't let me end it. Instead, he had a way of making me feel at ease and assured me that I'd never had to suck-up to anyone for any reason. I was quite the ornery, feisty, little rebel back then. He knew who I was and that's all that seemed to matter.

If I truly wanted this to work, it was up to me to save and stand up for myself. I was going to have to deal with life which now also included someone else's world.

A Glossy Exterior

We're born with what we are born with. No two are the same. From there we do with it what we may. One of the most dangerous things to do is to get attached to that exterior. No matter how much makeup, nip and tucking or injecting you do, your only guarantee is that it'll change over time.

Women carry double-edged swords in this regard. On the one hand, looks matter in a lot of industries like acting and your appearance can help open doors. On the flip side, it can intimidate and stir up insecurity in other people, both men, and women alike, and inadvertently be held against you. No matter how nice, kind, or generous you are, women are judged more harshly than men. We're our own worst critics, and ironically, the first to judge other females. Beautiful women are often viewed as dumb, air-headed, needing to be saved, and if they're with a man of power, often branded as gold diggers.

This is why it's so vitally important to come to terms with your inner queen. The one who knows that looks are only a small part of what makes her whole and that at the end of the day, has very little to do with how she rules her empire. Your sense of self-worth will trump any nip, tuck, injection or eyelash extension. If you don't already have a good baseline established about yourself, I encourage you to make that the very first thing you do.

It is knowing, owning, and rocking who you are underneath that pretty exterior which will come to your aid when you're faced with people who think otherwise. I'm not saying it's always easy, even the most self-assured among us will feel those foundations shake from time to time. But it is you who builds the foundation upon which you reign.

Mine for Gold

I saw a truly good man and my equal in Grant Cardone. For the first time, I recognized a man of comparable magnitude to me. A man that could actually handle me without trying to control me. That doesn't' happen every day and certainly never to me. I decided to do the very opposite thing that someone labeled a gold digger would do. I would go ahead and label myself a gold digger and actually mine for gold in Grant and in myself.

Even back then I saw Grant's potential. Not only in our relationship, but in himself and his business acumen. I knew it would be selfish to not share it with the world. He's happiest when he's producing and achieving his goals. If he doesn't have an outlet for his ferocious energy, the power can be misdirected. I've been caught in those crosshairs, and it's not fun. The best thing I could do as his girlfriend, and eventually his wife, was to always encourage him to continue to push, shove, and achieve those goals. The highest act of love you can give loved ones is to help them achieve their goals and dreams.

In other words, I embraced that **I am a gold digger**. It made me laugh at first. I was taking ownership of the very label that made my stomach turn, but it was true. I see the potential in people and in myself. I know that going for the gold is the only guarantee that you'll continue to learn and grow. It's certainly the only shot you've got at the metal.

The best part of it was I learned for the first time that I can combat others by empowering myself. It weakened their ability to have any power over me because I agreed with them. My mental game was forever changed. I learned that out of unwanted scenarios, I could flip a situation. I realized I could always maintain power or the upper hand if I just discovered a way.

California Scheming

I was fortunate in that Grant had shared what was going on behind the scenes with me. All of these people were talking very negatively about me behind my back. Their agenda? To break us up. But we were able to recognize what was happening and told these people to knock it off or get knocked off.

There are many relationships in which this dynamic happens. The man or woman, if not strong enough in their belief system, will eventually listen to their friends or family and dump the partner. The dumped partner is left in the dust, scratching their head and wondering what they did. Meanwhile, the friends/family members/ associates are gleeful when this happens because they have their friend or family member back.

By the way, I also had several friends who warned me about Grant. They were saying that Grant was a player and a shark, warning me that I better not let my guard down. Grant didn't seem phased by this either. I realized that if Grant and I were to stand a chance, we were going to have to trust each other and block out all the noise.

This change in attitude was what allowed my relationship with Grant to move forward and create the pathway for what it is today. Other people's words are just that, words. And while it pays to be successful, the biggest payout is having each other's back no matter what.

Start With Yourself

I mine for gold in myself every day of my life. Every single day, I'm pushing myself to learn, grow and expand. I try new things, and most importantly, get out of my comfort zone. I demand of myself the courage, honor, strength, and intelligence to strive for excellence.

You can't be willing to demand excellence from others if you don't first demand it of yourself. Coincidentally, it's the gold mining that will inspire others in your empire to become their best selves too. In other words, you're leading by example, not just from a podium with a loudspeaker. Then, and only then, can you demand gold from others, including your king. If someone has hustle in their muscle and a little love in their heart, then that's the gold I'll be mining. Those are the people and the energy I want to keep around me all day long.

Own Your Truth

Being called a gold digger, or any other name, stings and being caught in the throes of a family or friend dynamic can cause a lot of unnecessary drama and heartache. It causes a lot of unnecessary arguments in relationships if they're able to weather the storm at all. Empires that are not ironclad never survive.

If, on the other hand, you are gold digging, and looking for someone else to save you or being manipulative so you can get what you want without having to give, then I have no advice to offer. A true gold digger is an exceptional caliber of person who is committed to his or her own life and who wants to make a difference for the better. It has nothing to do with how much money you or your partner makes and has everything to do with what's in their heart. You can take away all the wealth and riches from a gold digger but you can never take away their identity. Their courage, dignity, pride, discipline, and dedication to greatness is the fabric of their soul. They don't need a car, plane or purse to make them a somebody. What's in the bank will never measure up to your inner wealth.

The luxuries are a mere symbol for a job well-done on both our behalf. They are just that; symbols of a reward. They do not define us or make us any better or worse as a human being. If all of our money went away, so be it. I still have honor, integrity, loyalty, courage, guts, commitment, determination, willingness to help others, love, creativity, passion, grit, intelligence, self-respect, dignity, pride and the list goes on and on. But these are the things that you have to mine and earn for yourself. Once you have discovered them, no one can ever take these away from you. They are your most powerful weapon and they are part of you!

Never give up looking for gold. You'll inevitably encounter rocks, whether they're negative people or self-doubt. Keep going. Have the faith that you'll find what you're looking for and know that you were already born with everything you could possibly need. You just need to discover it.

Empire-Building Exercise: Mine The Gold in Yourself

Now we've covered what gold-digging is, and isn't, it's time for you to mine for gold within yourself.

Make a list of your assets. Everything you have to offer others that you think benefits them. Some easy or obvious answers might be your ability to make other people laugh, that you're a tried and true friend or that you pay attention to the small details. Try to keep an open mind as you write, and don't judge if you write something that you feel is boastful or weird.

Once you're done with your list, set it aside, and pull out a fresh page. Now, begin to write down everything your partner does that's an asset to you or your relationship. If you're partnered, share your lists with each other and decide how you can bring your best selves to the table and continue to mine for gold as a couple.

If you're already mining for gold in each other — fantastic! Use this exercise as an opportunity to figure out how you can dig deeper and mine for more. Maybe there are tasks you need to delegate that will free up the energy and time to do this. Be ruthless in your assessment and plan of action.

You're on your way to becoming an unstoppable team. Unstoppable teams create empires. Empires create legacies which live forever.

Chapter 15

Your Empire Building Toolbox

This is your empire building toolbox.

Building an empire requires tools, but not the kind you'd necessarily pick up at the hardware store. Hard work, tenacity, grit and courage are the intangible things we all need in order to create anything in life worth having. When you're first starting out it can seem like these things are out of reach. I assure you, though if you dig deep enough inside of yourself, you can find the items you need in order to create the life, and empire of your dreams. Here's what you'll want to include in your empire building toolbox, including an exercise that'll remind you of where to find them when you're feeling lost.

P.S. None of these things costs a single dollar — just your spirit and willingness so you've got no excuses!

Awareness

It's simple, yet an important aspect of building an empire.

Wherever you go, whatever you do, and whoever you're with, you must be continuously aware of your surroundings and who is in it. This will affect how you approach challenges, successes, and the company you keep.

Commitment

When everything is on the line, and your back is against the wall, how committed to the cause are you? Building an empire requires an unwavering, can't-flinch commitment not just to your goals, but to yourself.

Discipline

None of us are born with discipline, rather, it develops over time. Think of it like depositing money at the bank. Every time you stick to something no matter how lazy, tired, or unmotivated you feel, whether it's making that extra call or going a literal extra mile on a run, you're signaling to your psyche <u>and</u> to the universe that you're not going anywhere. Not this time.

You build discipline by doing what you say. You start with small, simple challenges and you do it. You get it done no matter what. This builds your belief and confidence in yourself which develops your own personal sense of trust. This pays off later when you have to complete a task that is difficult to get done, or you hate, or are scared to do. It might be simply making the right decision when a temptation, which can come in any form, tries to lure you to the path of destruction. You will have trust in yourself and will use discipline to hold yourself accountable. It takes a strong and disciplined person to do the right thing.

Purpose

Why are you doing this? Who are you helping? What is your ultimate reason for being here? What is the mark you want to leave on this world? Knowing your purpose is your "why" that gives you the passion to fight for it all. Your purpose is what gives you the strength to rise up to your true potential and become the person you always envisioned yourself to be.

In other words, your purpose is your North Star. Never lose sight of it. Your purpose will give you the determination to put your pettiness, your selfish "wanting to quit" moments, the wanting to fight unnecessary battles aside and give you that extra ounce of grit to dig in, stay focused and push forward on your mission.

A Massive Action Plan

Empires aren't itty-bitty, they're huge. And they require massive, all-encompassing action. When it comes to mapping out your empire's reach, you've got to think big. Growth requires an element of discomfort, as well as detachment. In order to think bigger, you've got to act bigger and be bigger. That might require you to shed the image of yourself you've possibly held onto for far too long. Aligning to your purpose and values, especially if you're reaching bigger than you've ever done before, will provide additional assurance in times of growth. Massive action requires a bigger being to do more, and accomplish more. You must assume that you can do more than you thought and quit being small with small concepts about your abilities.

Observation

Study people. Not just what they say, but what they do, right down to how they speak, walk, to the condition of their property. Some might call it emotional intelligence. I call it a way to clue into what's going on beneath the surface. You can start with your inner circle. Or if you need to practice, go to a public space like a café or even a conference and see what you notice about how people interact with you, and with others. It might be helpful to bring along a notebook to record your observations, if only for your own benefit.

Knowing how to read people correctly will be a key tool in protecting your empire, especially when the stakes are high. You protect your empire by avoiding potential problematic people and unwanted situations. The more of these unwanted conditions you avoid, the faster you can grow. This pertains to everyone you hire, work next to, are friends with, and for some, even your family.

For the most part, people usually only measure their success based on what statistic they can physically see in terms of what they accomplished. However, I'll go on the record as counting and celebrating some of the biggest successes as being able to steer clear of the truly bad-intentioned individuals and situations. Do not underestimate your ability to perceive, based on not ignoring red flags, and having the certainty and courage in yourself to walk away from what appears to be a good deal. Every single time I thought something was too good to be true, it was. I have seen others lose millions, have their money stolen, go broke and even go to jail because they were blindly framed by criminals. There are no two ways around this, you have to develop this skill.

Your Personal Code of Conduct

How you carry yourself says everything about you. Yes, I'm partially talking about appearances here, but on a deeper level, I'm talking about values. You've got to get absolutely clear on what you will and will not stand for. You can also create a separate list of values with your spouse or partner to see what your code of conduct is as a family unit. Either way your personal code of conduct is like your operator's manual. When the check engine light of life goes on, you'll want to have it handy. It's important to not compromise your integrity so have this one mapped out. I don't care who you are, we all have temptations to take the easy route out. If you want to experience a good and happy life at the top, it's crucial you have clean hands. Be ethical.

Sacrifices

What are you willing to give up in order to have the empire you deserve? Every empire worth having comes with a cost. This can include:

BELIEFS - Old, outworn beliefs about money definitely will need to be addressed. If you have any prejudices toward people with money, confused ideas that money will somehow turn you into a bad person, or whatever type of things you tell yourself, it must go. You will self-sabotage yourself every single time.

If you want to build your empire, which includes building your finances, you will have to confront all the miscalculations you have about money. You need to declare what you want and not have any shame in going after it.

What are all the beliefs you have that are holding you back from the game of life? Look at all the opportunities you have, but always say no to by coming up with an excuse to not participate. Where you are completely set in your ways, is usually the place that needs to be changed immediately, at least to mix up the flow. You might think you can't hire anyone because you don't trust people, even if it is a much-needed accountant, housekeeper or babysitter. By not expanding so you can grow in other areas, you'll ultimately stay small if you are not acquiring more people into the fold.

When it comes to relationships or even the one you are in, look at what generalities you think about the opposite sex. What do you find yourself thinking about them? Do you have the notion that all men are no good? Or maybe the opposite and you are stereotyping women? What is that one belief that keeps you from finding your perfect match?

I could never be in a relationship before I met Grant because I believed men would hold me back in my career. Therefore, I had always dated guys that would do exactly that and subsequently, I always got to be right about my viewpoint. So my statement about guys was true for me.

I made a decision when I started dating Grant that maybe a man, and even relationships themselves, could actually lift me up and challenge me to great heights. It was a difficult concept but I kept that belief firm. Now, years later, he still continues to lift and challenge me to stretch myself to greater levels of success.

HABITS - Smoking, drinking, partying, sleeping in, staying out late or eating poorly doesn't fit into the scheme of building an empire.

Decide what you want more, Friday night cocktails and an expensive credit card tab, or your future freedom. Bottom line, you need a clear head and you can't afford to waste even a day on something as foolish as nursing a hangover.

PEOPLE - Not everyone in your inner circle gets a permanent seat just because they've always been there. This goes for family too. You aren't running the entitlement empire program here. It can feel harsh, even sad, to say goodbye to people, but they don't have your best interests at heart. When you put your purpose, integrity, and your empire first, the answers will come. When you create space, you make room for your royal court, the people who will ultimately help you build.

Some people will not want to see you do this. It's just a fact. They will try to make you feel guilty, like a sellout, or pull at your heartstrings to keep you the same "little old you" that they can keep comfortably fitted into their lives. These people who don't want to see you get better, have got to go! You can't expand by staying the same.

PLACES - Not all destinations are worth the drive. Whether it's a neighborhood bar, a casino, strip club, a dead-end city, or even a part of your home that drags you down, just say, *"No!"*

THINGS - Depending on where you are in life, this will be one of the easier sacrifices to make. If your TV isn't making you money, get rid of it, or at least put it out of sight. Household clutter, junk, a wardrobe that doesn't contribute to a positive first impression — clear it out for good. On this same note, don't get accustomed to a fancy lifestyle before you've put in the time. Building an empire isn't about having the latest and greatest technology, designer clothes or a fancy car.

Counsel

Let your financial advisor be your financial advisor. Let your mechanic be your mechanic. Let your kid's teacher be your kid's teacher. An expert in their field should know their subject matter cold. Skip their advice when it comes to everything else. These experts are NOT the expert on how to run your life so don't take advice from them. The financial advisor doesn't know how to run your family. The teacher doesn't know how to run a multi-million-dollar empire. I know it sounds harsh but only listen to the expert that has the proven stat in that field IF you so choose. Learn to trust in yourself, and your partner, for the most important matters.

I try not to open the door to unwanted discussions with people who do not qualify to give me advice. However, from time to time they like to offer it anyway. In these cases, I usually just smile and say, *"thank you."* This does not mean I take the advice or agree. I am simply getting out of the conversation. There is no need for me to spend any time trying to argue or defend my position. It would only act as a distraction that wastes time which I don't have to spare.

Your Court

The people who surround you aren't just your friends and coworkers, they're assets. They make up an important factor of what your empire will look like. Be selective about who you spend time with, both on and offline, and make sure your court knows how valuable they are to you. Spend what extra time you have acquiring real, loyal friends/assets who will be there to help and defend you and your family if ever you need and vice versa.

Yourself

Reach for the crown because YOU are your greatest asset, worthy of pouring in and investing with every iota of your soul, time, energy and your money. Always, always, always work on yourself. Push, learn, grow, and expand. An asset provides value to oneself and to others. Before you build an empire, before feed your family, before you support your spouse, you must take care of you. Don't skimp on the most important tool in your toolbox. Rest, eat well, exercise, surround yourself with people of integrity, and stay focused on your targets. Become the asset that others can depend on, and who others want to protect.

Laugh, Have Fun & Play Games

Laughter, having fun and playing games are underestimated tools that are an absolute MUST HAVE in the toolbox arsenal. It seems like all I have mentioned so far is how challenging this empire thing is and how focused one must remain in order to accomplish the goals. Although that might be true, none of it would be worth it if life was so serious that it sucked all the joy from it. The more intense life can be, the more you MUST incorporate the fun. It helps to blow off the steam and gets your head right so you can get back in the game with a fresh perspective.

Grant and I chose to live in the pressure cooker of life. We have big goals and we understand that life is continuously serving up challenges that never seem to let up. Not even for that sometimes much-wanted break. The fun is what gets us through the times until we get awarded the trophy of a victory. We know life is a game and we remind ourselves not to get so wrapped up in it that we forget we are PLAYING. Sometimes the more fun it looks like we are having is actually a gauge to exactly how intense it really is!

Don't misunderstand me, I am not talking about stupid fun. That fun is actually a liability and actually costs you. For every hour you wasted destroying, you must add that time on the back end of what you allotted for your target attainment. You might even need to double or triple the time depending on how severe the bad decisions you made while under the influence of that fun time.

What I am talking about is good clean fun. The fun we have every day with each other, going out of the way to make each other laugh or smile. Grant and I find ways to turn everything into a game, which then turns into a competition to see who will win. It's usually me! We are always having a blast together. It makes our lives interesting and breaks up the normal, monotonous routine that sometimes can creep in.

It's about the fun you force yourself to have when you show up and participate in life. You will be amazed at what opportunities life presents when you just lighten up a bit!

Empire-Building Exercise: What's In Your Toolbox?

Now that you have a basic idea of the essential empire building tools, put them into your own toolbox — literally! Draw, write or sketch out your tools. What does your toolbox look like? Write out who are you and who you would like to become. What are the strengths and weaknesses? Who is currently in your life? Who do you want in your life? What do you need to give up or do more of? What is your purpose, your mission? Who do you want to help? What are some policies you can put in place going forward that will help you stay on course? What can you do to have more good, clean fun? Where can you go out of your way to make others laugh?

If you've got additional tools that'll serve your empire, include them here. What are your strong suits? Where are you slacking? What do you need more of? How do you improve that area? Make a plan and strengthen a weakness or find ways to avoid them. Keep your strong suit polished and ready for battle.

This toolbox will be yours to refer to when you need help getting through a tough spot.

Chapter 16

Beyond Your Empire: Your Legacy

At the end of your life, your empire has two options:

1. It ends when you do; or
2. It continues to live on without your physical presence.

For many people, option one is the norm. They live by the rules society has set out for them. They go to school, get married, pick a safe job, aim for a few kids and a white picket fence, maybe go on a few vacations, try to retire by 65 and try to not cause too big of a stir. Nothing ever really changes. Nothing ever really grows. Everything within their world is small, but they're seemingly OK with it. At least that's what they'll tell you if you challenge them on it. These are people who might have had the potential to build great empires at one point in their lives, but instead, they settled on easy street. They never really pushed the boundaries of how far life could take them.

Option two is a bit different. Think about family businesses that are built, grown, and passed down from generation to generation. These aren't just companies. They're iron-clad empires, carefully built over the years to weather many storms, to survive and thrive into the future indefinitely. These are the people whose funerals are packed due to all of the lives they've touched, and whose name is never forgotten. These are two quite different outcomes, and of course, two great extremes.

But there's a reason why you chose this book. You know there's something special inside of you that's been waiting to come out. You know you have what it takes to build something great. An empire. And you're ready and willing to put the work in to make it happen. Maybe you're already on your way to building an empire or want to take your empire to the next level. The question I want to leave you with is, when?

When is it ever the right time to try something new? When do you invest back into yourself, your family, your community? When do you recognize that you are a queen or king and that you deserve to live a life fit for one? When do you create your empire or enhance your existing one?

The answer is now. Now is the right time to get started on your goals and to commit yourself to the highest version of you possible. Now is the time to go all in on yourself and your empire. Now is when you start creating your legacy to leave a positive imprint on other people's lives that will forever leave you immortalized in the future.

No one likes to think about death, yet so many of us live like we're already dead. We wrongly assume that if we just keep doing what we're doing, that everything will eventually work itself out. Or that the magic lottery ticket will suddenly appear, or that someone will come in to save us from whatever unwanted condition we've created ourselves.

Here's what happens when you keep your head down for too long though, life will pass you by. It won't stop and tap you on the shoulder to ask if you're having fun, or if you're achieving your goals, or if you're living the life you always dreamed of as a kid. Instead, the clock will continue to tick, the days will continue to pass, and one day you'll wake up wondering how you're still in that same dead-end job, relationship or neighborhood. Take your pick. All because you never took a chance on yourself. The past is done with, but it leaves clues as to what remains to be done. Only you can create an empire worthy of admiration and respect. Only you can decide in which direction you want to steer your ship.

If there's anything I want to leave you with, it's to think really, really big. Give yourself the gift of imagining that there's another way to exist in this great world of ours, and remember that one of the greatest gifts you can give to it is by showing up as your biggest, most badass self.

So come forth, kings and queens. History awaits you.

Empire-Building Exercise: Write Your Obituary

Press pause and imagine that today was your last day on earth. How would your obituary read? Would it include everything you'd hoped to achieve and the names of people and organizations touched by your efforts? Or would it resemble that of someone who never really showed up, and let life happen to them?

Now, imagine that it's ten, twenty, thirty, heck, even a hundred years from now and you had accomplished everything that you ever imagined for yourself. How would people talk about you after you've passed on? What sort of contributions would your empire have provided to this world?

Write out both obituaries. Then, compare them. What do you need to do to ensure your legacy lives on long after you? It's easy to say, while you're still alive, that you're going to do all of these great things. It's another to actually take action and do them!

Start. Build an Empire!

Acknowledgments

No one builds an empire alone, and this book wouldn't be possible without my royal court.

To my Mom: Thank you for your never-ending support, love, and patience. Lord knows I certainly tested its limits in my heyday. Thank you for setting the framework for what it takes to be an excellent mother and for always being there for me. You are the kindest and most loving mother who I can always depend on.

To my Father, may you rest in peace: You were the best father a daughter could wish for.

Thank you beyond words for all that you taught me about life and for the belief and encouragement to chase my dreams. It was an honor to be a Daddy's girl.

To my husband, my life partner, King Grant Cardone: You make the world, and my life, an infinitely better place by being in it. You have patiently stood by my side without judgment as I figure this thing called life and myself out. You have always delivered and never let me down. I'm so thankful for all that you do and for who you are. You are a mentor to me and I am, and always will be, your biggest fan.

To my daughters, Sabrina and Scarlett: Thank you for reminding me about the endless potential we all have inside of ourselves and for continuing to inspire me every day. It's a gift and honor to be your mother. Thank you for trusting me with the job. I look forward to watching you grow up and I can't wait to see where life takes both of you. I will always be your mother, on your side, and also a true friend and ally whenever you need me.

To my sister, Cece, who's creativity and individuality to be herself as she forges through life, traveling the world multiple times over, has inspired me to do the same.

To Sheri Hamilton, Supernova Chief Operating Officer, and Superwoman Empress: You are a miracle worker, times a million, and an absolute queen. I love, adore, appreciate and value you so very much. Thank you for ALWAYS having my six.

To the team at Grant Cardone Enterprises: Thank you for your unwavering commitment to our higher cause, to the company, and to becoming your own personal best. You guys just kick ass. Thanks for always showing up ready to 10X.

To my best friends from New Orleans: Stephanie LeBon, Rebecca Nordgren, Stacy Tucker and Christy Connelly. Whether it's us against the Big Easy or us against the world, you remind me of what it means to be confident, poised, and simply wonderful women. We witnessed it all and protect our own. You are my girls for life, true ride or die chicks. Level 1, First Tier.

To Diego De Vera, my sensei, master instructor and owner of KO Zone in Miami Beach: Thanks for giving me a place to call home and for being someone I can not only count on, but can also call a true friend. Your patience and willingness to teach me have given me an immeasurable sense of self-confidence and courage. You empower any woman who wants to empower themselves and I admire that. You are tough but you are fair. You treat everyone with the respect. You prepare and train me to take all of life's punches — quite literally too. See you in the ring. Fight2Death.

To my shooting instructors: Thank you. Training with you is an honor and I learn something new with every shot. Lesgar Murdock Jr. AKA Speedy, Farewell Firearms: Joe Farewell, RealWorld Tactical: Tony Sentmanat, KO Zone: Diego De Vera, Luigi Li, Bat Defense: Jeff Cotto, Colby Allen, Ray Chirnside, Ashleigh Gass, Taran Tactical: Taran Butler.

To our armed forces, all branches of the active and retired military and first responders: I salute you. I am so incredibly humbled and grateful for your service. Thank you for being the warrior heroes that you, and your families are to this beautiful country of ours. Words will never be enough to express my appreciation of your courage to maintain our freedoms. God Bless America.

To D.M., I salute you Sir. Thank you.

And finally, to our legion of loyal fans on all social mediums, those who tune in each week to the G&E Show, and the bold dreamers who make their way to the 10X Growth Conference each year: Keep building your empires. Your spirit, encouragement, positivity, and your successes make this journey all the more enjoyable—and whether we've met in person or if it's in the future, I hope this book inspires you to go be the real you! No dream is too big. So get out there and 10X it. I always love and appreciate your support.

Follow me on Instagram and other social media @ElenaCardone and at Facebook.com/ElenaCardoneWIP.

Resources

Building an empire is a lifelong, day-by-day, process. And as we talked about in the book, it's a journey best taken in good company. The following resources have helped me in building my own empire, and might also be of service to you. Ultimately, it's up to each of us to explore, stretch, and conquer until you find the people, places, and practices best suited to help you live a 10X life.

The G&E Show

GrantCardoneTV.com/channel/geshow

Each Wednesday at 12pm EST, Grant and I tackle the business of marriage, and what we do to make it all work. As we say, *"We're not perfect, but we're figuring it out."*

Tune in on GCTV.com, or on iTunes - Cardone Zone, Stitcher or YouTube.

One-On-One Coaching with Elena Cardone

GrantCardone.com/Elena

Want to go beyond building a basic empire? I offer one-on-one coaching with highly-motivated individuals who want to set and achieve their personal goals so that they can take their lives and empires to 10X levels.

Coaching packages include:

• One-on-one, face-to-face meetings with me personally in Miami, or via phone/Skype for long-distance and international clients.

• Working directly together in person, or by phone, to map out your empire step-by-step. Where it starts, how big you want it to be, who's going to be in it, what the rules are and what you'll do to protect it.

• Create achievable, workable strategies to CRUSH all of life's biggest obstacles.

• Build your confidence, intuition, and public speaking skills—on and off the camera.

Grant Cardone: Coaching, Books, Sales and Career Training, and the 10X Growth Conference

GrantCardone.com

Bestselling author of The 10X Rule, Sell or Be Sold, Closer's Survival Guide, Millionaire Booklet, If You Aren't First You're Last, Be Obsessed or Be Average and How to Create Wealth Investing in Real Estate. Real estate investor, entrepreneur and motivational speaker, Grant Cardone is my husband and emperor.

He is a sales genius and has helped millions of people worldwide achieve the success they otherwise could only dream of. He has a number of programs, including sales training, books, audiobooks, podcasts and, of course, the 10X Growth Conference which is designed to help anyone achieve 10X levels.

Visit GrantCardone.com or CardoneCapital.com to learn more, and follow him on Facebook at GrantCardoneFan and across social media @GrantCardone.

For non-accredited investors, this is a solicitation of an indication of interest. No solicitation or acceptance of money or other consideration, nor of any commitment, binding or otherwise, from any person is permitted until qualification of the offering statement.

About Elena Cardone

 Elena Cardone started her career in Hollywood and soon became a successful actress and model of TV and film fame. A lifelong competitive sport shooter, and now author, businesswoman, public speaker, empire builder and visionary, Elena currently hosts her own show "Women in Power" and co-hosts "The G&E Show" with her husband, Grant Cardone, bestselling author, entrepreneur and real estate investor. Together they have created a real estate portfolio of almost one-billion dollars.

Born in Spain and raised in New Orleans, this 2004 Maxim Magazine's Hottest 100 beauty now spends her time serving as Chief Family Officer, public speaker and personal development coach teaching others the strategies and techniques on how to create, build and expand their personal empires everywhere.

Elena is an avid human rights activist and strong supporter of constitutional and civil rights. As a mother, she is also a fierce advocate for parental rights such as informed consent and the right to protect one's children from harm. A busy philanthropist, she campaigns cross-country tirelessly.

Elena has been happily married since 2004 (July 4th to be exact – and the fireworks have never stopped) and lives with her husband Grant and their two daughters, Sabrina and Scarlett in Miami Beach.

Follow Elena on Instagram and Twitter @ElenaCardone, and on Facebook at Facebook.com/ElenaCardoneWIP.